N. Matson

Pioneers of Illinois

containing a series of sketches relating to events that occured previous to 1813

N. Matson

Pioneers of Illinois
containing a series of sketches relating to events that occured previous to 1813

ISBN/EAN: 9783337095987

Printed in Europe, USA, Canada, Australia, Japan

Cover: Foto ©ninafisch / pixelio.de

More available books at **www.hansebooks.com**

PIONEERS OF ILLINOIS

CONTAINING

A SERIES OF SKETCHES

RELATING TO

EVENTS THAT OCCURRED PREVIOUS TO 1813;

ALSO

NARRATIVES OF MANY THRILLING INCIDENTS CONNECTED WITH
THE EARLY SETTLEMENT OF THE WEST,

DRAWN FROM

HISTORY, TRADITION AND PERSONAL REMINISCENCES.

BY N. MATSON,

AUTHOR OF "BEYOND THE ATLANTIC," "REMINISCENCES OF BUREAU
COUNTY," "FRENCH AND INDIANS OF ILLINOIS RIVER,"
"MEMORIES OF SHAUBENA," ETC.

CHICAGO:
KNIGHT & LEONARD, PRINTERS.
1882.

PREFACE.

IN presenting these pages to the public it becomes necessary to make a few plain statements in order that the reader may understand the purposes of the writer. The object of collecting the early traditions of the country has been for the purpose of supplying the many missing links in history, and also to correct some of its errors. To gather these materials has been attended with much labor, the work of more than forty years, and various means of obtaining facts have been resorted to. In these researches many new items have been developed, errors in history corrected, but the work of harmonizing all conflicting statements has not been an entire success.

While the Indians were still in the country I had frequent interviews with them, and listened to their accounts of events which had come down through many generations. In order to obtain more of their early history I employed an educated half-breed of western Kansas to collect traditions among his people, especially of those whose ancestors formerly lived along the Illinois River.

At different times I visited the descendants of the early French pioneers now living on the American Bottom, and heard their stories of past events which had come down through the third and fourth generations. I also visited places of early historical renown, at some of which relics of the past can still be seen, and the descriptions herein given of these localities are drawn from personal observations. Many of the incidents narrated in this book were obtained from persons who figured in them, and every statement not well authenticated has been excluded from these pages.

An account of the early French exploration of Illinois has been given in almost every county history in the state, consequently I would like to omit this part entirely, but it cannot be done without doing injustice to the work. Therefore in giving a short sketch of these events, compiled from history, I have added some of the French and Indian traditions relating thereto. These items have been collected at different times from various sources, compared and revised with much care, and for the first time given to the public.

A few years ago I published two editions of a book entitled "French and Indians of Illinois River," relating to the same subject as this, and many of the incidents given in that volume have been revised, corrected, and inserted in this one.

N. M.

CONTENTS.

CHAPTER I.

ANTIQUITIES OF ILLINOIS.

The Mammoth and the Mastodon.— Topography of Illinois River.— Illinois Indians.— Massacre of Indians.— Raid of the Iroquois. - 17

CHAPTER II.

Father Marquette.— Discovery of the Mississippi River.— The Voyageurs at La Vantum. 28

CHAPTER III.

The cross raised on the bank of Chicago River.— Mission of Immaculate Conception.— Death of Marquette.— Resurrecting of Marquette's bones. - - - - - - 38

CHAPTER IV.

La Vantum, or great Illinois town.— The great Western explorer.— La Salle and friends western bound.— French at Peoria Lake.— Fort Crève-Cœur. - - - - - 48

CHAPTER V.

La Salle in the Indian camp.— Henri de Tonti.— The French at La Vantum.— Reception of evil tidings.— Battle and Massacre. - 59

CHAPTER VI.

Torturing prisoners.— Death of Father Gabriel.— A Scene of Horror.— Starved Rock. - 72

CHAPTER VII.

Building of Fort St. Louis.—Trade with the Indians.—La Salle's success, failure and death.—Fort St. Louis attacked by Iroquois.—Return of Tonti's victorious army. · 83

CHAPTER VIII.

La Fort des Miamis.—The last of Tonti.—Fort St. Louis burned and colony broken up. Chassagoac, an Indian Chief.—Louisiana Colony.—French settlement around Fort St. Louis. - - - - - - - 93

CHAPTER IX.

Jesuit Missionary of the West.—Father Senat and comrades burned at the stake.— Early French settlement of Illinois.—Early settlement of St. Louis.— British rule in Illinois. 107

CHAPTER X.

Tom Brady's wild adventure.—Two expeditions against St. Joseph and one against Detroit.— Pat Kennedy and comrades in search of copper mines. - - - - 119

CHAPTER XI.

Colonel Clark's conquest of Illinois. - - 127

CHAPTER XII.

Pontiac.— An error in history.— Massacre of a hunting party.— The Ottawas ordered out of the country.— The Indian council.— Pontiac assassinated.—A war of extermination. 137

CHAPTER XIII.

Rock of refuge.—The besiegers and besieged.—Various traditionary evidence.— A ghastly spectacle. - - - - - - - 153

CHAPTER XIV.

Relics of the tragedy.— Searching for gold.— Fort St. Louis.— Rock Fort and Le Rocher.— Relics of Fort St. Louis.— Indians and French relics.—Father Buche's manuscript. 166

CHAPTER XV.

Fort Massac.— American Bottom.— Prairie du Rocher.— Cahokia.— Kaskaskia.— Kaskaskia and Cahokia Indians.— Peoria Indians. 180

CHAPTER XVI.

Indian tribes in Illinois territory.— Monks of La Trappe.— Old fort near Starved Rock.— The ruined city of Aztalan.— Ancient fortification of Marseilles.— The ruined fort on Fox River.—Medore Jennette, a fur trader. 193

CHAPTER XVII.

English and French relations with Indians.— American Pioneers of Illinois.— Early government of Illinois.— Disappearing of buffalo.— Early history of Chicago.— Jean Baptiste and Father Bonner. - - - 205

CHAPTER XVIII.

Early settlement at Peoria.— La ville de Millet. French inhabitants of Peoria.—French costumes and manners.— French land claims. - 115

CHAPTER XIX.

Pierre De Beuro, an Indian trader.—Tecumseh at Peoria.— Indian depredations.— Indian council at Cahokia.— Illinois territory at the time of the British war.— A false report circulated. - - - - - - - 229

CHAPTER XX.

Black Partridge, a noted Indian chief.—Indians receiving the first tidings of war.— Mrs. Helm's life saved by Black Partridge.— Emissaries from Tecumseh.—Unjust retribution. - - - - - - - - 243

CHAPTER XXI.

Lieutenant Helm ransomed by Black Partridge. —Mrs. Basson's narrative.—The French at Peoria regarded as enemies.— Captain Craig's account of his attack on Peoria.— Burning of Peoria.— Domestic animals left by the captives. - - - - - - 254

CHAPTER XXII.

Indian raid on the settlement.— Captivity of Amanda Wolsey.— General Howard's expedition against the Indians.— Black Partridge with his braves in defense of their country. — Colonel Davenport's account of the block house. - - - - - - - 274

CHAPTER XXIII.

Building of Fort Clark.—Indians collect on Bureau.— Lieutenant Robenson in search of the enemy.— Treaty of peace. - - - 284

CHAPTER XXIV.

Descendants of the French settlers at Peoria.— Perils of fur traders.— Burning of Fort Clark. - - - - - - - 293

CHAPTER I.

ANTIQUITIES OF ILLINOIS.

ARTIFICIAL mounds are found everywhere throughout the western country, but are more numerous along the Illinois River and its tributaries. These mounds vary in size, shape and general formation. Some of them are only small elevations, called sepulchral mounds, in which are found human bones and different kinds of trinkets. Others are of various forms, representing the figure of a man, birds, animals, turtles, alligators, etc. Some of these mounds, from appearance, were intended for fortifications, others for sacramental purposes, and many of them the object for which they were constructed cannot be determined.

Mounds and earthworks are generally found near the present center of wealth and activity, showing that the ancient race understood the advantage of locality as well as people of the present day do. These mounds are only found where the soil is rich, the scenery fine, and near large streams of water, but never appear in a poor, barren country. The mounds found throughout the west have been classified as fortifications, temples, altars, sepulchers, signal stations and symbolic figures.

Some of the small mounds may have been the work of Indians, and of comparative recent date, but the large ones undoubtedly belong to the prehistoric age, and built by people who have long since passed away. Among the largest of this class of mounds is Mount Monk, on the American Bottom, and Mount Joliet, on the Des Plaines River, near the city of Joliet. The former at the base is eight hundred yards in circumference and ninety feet high. The latter nearly one mile in circumference and one hundred and fifty feet high, rising like a great pyramid in the midst of a plain. Some people believe these large mounds were formed by some freak of nature, therefore the subject of their formation belongs to geology rather than history. Others regard the mound builders as a myth, the offspring of fanatical antiquists claiming that nature and Indians did these works. But these skeptics are not posted in relation to the many thousand works of this kind found in the Mississippi Valley, which it must be admitted have been made by human hands, and could not have been the work of Indians. Who built these mounds, at what time, and for what purpose, opens a field of wild speculation. On this subject men of science have advanced many curious opinions without establishing any reliable facts.

There are many speculative theories advanced relating to the ancient people who at one time inhabited this country, but this mystery is buried in the unknown past, where in all probability it will forever remain. Who these people were, from whence they came, and what became of them, are questions often asked, but never satisfactorily answered. In the absence of any knowledge of these people, and for the want of a better and more appropriate name, they are called Mound Builders. The cities built and temples erected by these people (if any) have long since disappeared, and the marvels alone remain to tell the story of the past. Unlike the ancient Egyptians they have left no monumental obelisks covered with hieroglyphics, nor a rosetta stone, as a key to the mysteries of past ages.

A great deal of nonsense, under the name of science, has been written by late antiquarians in relation to mounds and mound builders without throwing any light on the subject.

Some remarkable facts relating to antiquities in this section of the country will be found in another part of this book under the head of ancient fortifications and ruined cities.

THE MAMMOTH AND THE MASTODON.

At one time the **gigantic mammoth** and **mastodon** roamed at large over the prairies of Illinois, and left their bones in many places, sunk deep in the marshes. At what time these monsters inhabited this country, what their form, movements, and habits were, the time and cause of disappearance, will in all probability forever remain a mystery. Skeletons of different species of these animals have been exhumed from swamps and marshes in a good state of preservation, and now adorn the museums of this country. Many facts have been collected which leave no doubt that people lived in this country when these animals roamed at large. In exhuming the bones of one of these monsters some years ago near Beardstown, an arrow-head and a broken point of a copper spear were found among the bones, showing that the beast came to its death by the hand of man. Dr. Koch, who has supplied foreign museums with skeletons of mastodons from this western country, says: In exhuming the bones of one of these animals from a marsh where it had mired the skeleton was found, standing erect. A fire had been kindled against it, and ashes, pieces of charred wood, with arrow-heads, stone axes and other weapons, were found among the bones, showing conclusively in what way the beast came to its death.

In 1773 James Douglass, the first white man that visited Big Bone Lick, in Kentucky, found a large number of mammoth bones lying on top of the ground in a good state of preservation. Some of the rib bones he set upright, and spread a blanket on them, forming a tent to shelter him from rain and sun.

According to tradition, at the time of the early French exploration of this country many large bones were found at a lick a short distance from Peoria Lake, and among them were two tusks ten feet in length. In the early settlement of this country large bones were occasionally found on top of the ground which could not have belonged to any animal known at the present time. As a rule bones on top of the ground will last only about fifty years, but instances are on record where they have remained sound after lying for many ages.

Bones of the mammoth and mastodon are found everywhere on this continent, but in greater numbers in the Valley of the Mississippi, but neither history nor tradition has left any account of them in a living state. These animals, judging from their bones, must have been of an enormous size; the elephant of the present time in comparison to them would be a mere pigmy. The skeleton of one of these, now in the museum of the University at Rochester, N. Y., is sixteen feet high, twenty-six feet in length, with tusk fourteen feet long, and at the base one foot in diameter.

In the spring of 1881 the bones of one of these monsters were found embedded in a slough two miles northeast of Princeton. Although the bones were much decayed, and not enough of them remained to form a skeleton, it is believed the animal to have been about fifteen feet high, and twenty-two feet in length.

TOPOGRAPHY OF THE ILLINOIS RIVER.

From the junction of the Kankakee with Des Plaines to the mouth of Illinois River, exclusive of windings, is two hundred and sixty miles, two hundred and ten miles of which is navigable for steamboats. The Illinois is a sluggish stream; in two hundred miles it has only twenty-eight feet fall, about the amount of fall necessary for canal navigation, and when the Mississippi is high it backs up the Illinois River seventy-two miles. The river bottom is from one to two miles wide, but at Beardstown it is twelve miles between the bluffs. The bottom lands are about equally divided between timber and prairie. The soil very rich, but much of it subject to inundation. The bluffs are from one to two hundred feet high, and mostly covered with timber. At Starved Rock, and also at Marseilles, are extensive rapids, with a wide, shallow channel interspersed with many beautiful wood-clad islands.

The scenery along the Illinois River is very beautiful; the broad stream dotted here and there with islands has attracted the attention and received the admiration of both savage and civilized people. The river banks are made attractive by alternate timber and prairie, and passes through a fertile country, which in former times abounded in game. For the possession of this country, according to tradition, has caused many a hard-fought battle, between savage tribes, and the bones of the victors as well as the vanquished have been left to decay on its banks.

On the bank of the Illinois River the French established the first canony in the Mississippi Valley, and here a nucleus was formed for settling the Great West. In former times its placid waters were navigated only by the bark canoes of savages, after which the little bateaux of the French were seen on its waters for about one hundred and forty years. These crafts, loaded with furs, and sails spread to the breeze, passed up the river from French villages, coasting along the lakes to Canada, and return with goods for the Indian market. At a later period the Mackinaw boat of the American Fur Company took the place of French bateaux. Following in the wake of these crafts came the sluggish keel boat, loaded with emigrants, which in their turn disappeared on the introduction of steam navigation.

ILLINOIS INDIANS.

The Illinois Indians were of the Algonquin family, and consisted of five bands or semi-tribes, named as follows: Kaskaskias, Cahokias, Peorias, Tamaroas and Michigamies. The three former bands occupied villages bearing their respective names, and the two latter the country north of Peoria Lake. According to the statement of early French explorers, these Indians were the most numerous of all the tribes of the west, occupying almost the entire territory now included within the State of Illinois. Along the Mississippi and Illinois Rivers, from the mouth of Ohio to Lake Michigan, their villages were found at short intervals, and the vast country east and west of these rivers was their hunting-grounds. Over this country herds of buffalo, elk and deer roamed for their benefit, and the many rivers were navigated only by their bark canoes. From the many groves the smoke from their camp-fires was seen to ascend, and the lonely forest reëchoed their wild war whoops. These Indians had many towns on the Illinois River, the largest and most important one, called La Vantum, located near the present site of Utica, an account of which will be given in the succeeding chapter.

On account of abundance of game (Illinois being known as the buffalo country), neighboring tribes frequently made this their hunting-ground, and although the Illinois Indians were not a warlike people, still they would resent an encroachment on their rights, consequently many bloody battles were fought with the aggressors.

More than a century ago the northern bands of the Illinois Indians became extinct, therefore most of their traditions are lost, still there are some things relating to them preserved by the French pioneers which are related by their descendants now living on the American Bottom.

MASSACRE OF INDIANS.

According to tradition, there was a large Indian village on the east side of the Illinois River, a short distance above the head of Peoria Lake. Near this village, on the bank of the river and partly surrounded by a bayou, was a place where the Indians held their annual religious feasts. On this ground was erected an altar, containing images of the different gods, and around which the Indians knelt in prayer while offering up sacrifices. At one of these feasts all the warriors of the village and many from neighboring ones were collected here engaged in religious exercises, while squaws and papooses stood looking on, and mingling their voices in songs of praise. The warriors, dispossessed of their arms, were engaged in devotion, the priests exhorting them in the ways of holiness, and receiving their annual offerings. While thus engaged they were suddenly attacked by a large body of Pottawatomies and most of them slain. Being taken by surprise, and unarmed, defense or escape appeared impossible, and many a brave warrior sang his death song and submitted to his fate. A few escaped by swimming the river, but the most of them, including squaws and papooses, fell an easy prey to the victorious enemy.

The victors collected all the valuables of the vanquished, including arms, clothing, camp equipage, furs, pelts, etc., loading them on ponies, and with their spoils left for their homes on the Wabash.

The date of this tragical affair is not known, but it was before the advent of the French, or the raids on these Indians by the Iroquois. For some time after the French came to this country the ground where this massacre took place was strewn with human bones.

RAID OF THE IROQUOIS.

The Iroquois Indians from the east made frequent raids on the Illinoisans, destroying their towns, killing squaws and papooses, and carrying away large quantities of pelts, furs, etc., which they sold to English traders. According to tradition, in one of those raids they carried off eight hundred prisoners, mostly squaws and papooses, and burned them at their village on the bank of Seneca Lake. The Iroquois, having been in trade with the English at Albany, had armed themselves with rifles, which gave them great advantage over the Illinoisans, who used bows and arrows only. These frequent raids of the Iroquois were for spoil only, and not for conquest, as they made no effort to take possession of the country. The Illinoisans were rich in ponies, furs, pelts, trinkets, etc., and the robbers would return loaded with spoil, and at one time they brought back three hundred ponies loaded with valuables. It is said the traders at Albany encouraged these robberies by furnishing the Iroquois with war implements, and buying the stolen goods.

On account of the frequent raids on the Illinoisans they became reduced in numbers, which caused them to fall an easy prey to the neighboring tribes some years afterward. A little over a century ago a number of tribes combined, forming an alliance against the Illinois Indians, which resulted in their annihilation, and the occupation of the country by the victors, as will be shown in the sequel.

CHAPTER II.

FATHER MARQUETTE.

A FEW years ago, while passing through the vatican at Rome, my attention was called to a department entitled "Portraits of North American Jesuits." On entering this department I noticed a life-sized portrait of a man in the garb of a priest, with an open bible in his hands and a gold cross on his breast. This portrait represented a man in the prime of life, tall and well proportioned, with handsome moulded features, and a countenance beaming with intelligence. Below this picture was a motto in Latin, and also the name of Father Jacques Marquette, a Jesuit priest of North America.

Marquette was born at Leon, in the north part of France, of a wealthy and distinguished family. He was of fine personal appearance, a strong intellect, well educated, and, while young, became a magnet in his native city. At a proper age he was ordained a priest, and being enthusiastic about the conversion of heathens he sailed for America, forsaking home, friends and wealth to spend a life among savages in the New World. After remaining a short time at Quebec Marquette went west to Lake Huron, where he spent a number of years among the Indians, instructing them in the ways of Christianity. While among these Indians he learned their languages, and it is said that he understood, and could speak, six different Indian dialects.

Marquette went to Sault Ste. Marie, where Father Allouez had established a mission, and for a time traveled through the country visiting different tribes of Indians, and among them made converts wherever he went. His active spirit could not rest, causing him to travel from place to place exposed to inclement weather. wading through water and snow, spending days without shelter or fire, subsisting on parched corn, or moss gathered from rocks, sometimes paddling his canoe up and down streams, or along the lake shore, and sleeping at night in open air. Said Marquette in a letter to a friend in France: "A life in the wilderness has its charms, and the rude hut of a savage is better adapted to a true disciple of Christ than the palace of a king. My heart ofttimes swells with rapture as my canoe glides over strange waters, or while plodding my way through thick forests, among briers and thorns, in laboring for the cause of my Redeemer."

Father Marquette founded a mission at Point

St. Ignace, opposite the island of Mackinaw, and Indians from different villages along the lake came thither for religious instruction. He built here on the bank of the lake a small chapel, dedicated to St. Ignace, and a few years afterward was buried beneath its altar.

DISCOVERY OF THE MISSISSIPPI RIVER.

For many years Indians from the far west, while visiting French trading posts in Canada, spoke of a great river that flowed into the ocean, but the course of this river and where it discharged its waters could not be learned. However, it was generally believed to empty into the Pacific Ocean, and through it a water communication could be obtained across the continent. The Governor of Canada, knowing the great advantage to be derived from this outlet to the west, selected Louis Joliet, a Canadian by birth, to make the necessary discovery.

In the spring of 1673 Joliet was furnished with the necessary outfit for the voyage, and prepared himself to embark in this hazardous enterprise. Father Marquette, having acquired much fame among the natives on the shore of Lake Huron, was selected to accompany this expedition. This priest being an earnest votary of the Virgin Mary, and to do her bidding he was willing to make any sacrifice.

His bold nature knew no fear, and he was prepared to suffer all deprivations, endure all hardships in discovering new lands and conquering new realms, to the honor and glory of her holiness. Before starting on his journey he wrote to a friend at Quebec saying: "In making this voyage I place myself under the protection of the Holy Virgin, and if she grants me the privilege of seeing the great river of the west, and follow its course to the Pacific Ocean, I will name it to her honor The Immaculate Conception."

All things being ready, Joliet and Marquette, accompanied by five companions, in two bark canoes, started on their journey. They carried with them a supply of smoked meat and Indian corn, besides a great variety of trinkets as presents to the Indians.

After a tempestuous voyage in coasting along the shore of Lake Michigan, they arrived at Green Bay early in May. After giving the natives many presents, and accompanied by an Indian guide, they continued on their way westward. While rowing their canoes up the rapid current of Fox River they reached a village on its banks whose inhabitants advised them to go no farther on their journey, or their lives would be sacrificed. They told the voyageurs that the banks of the great river were inhabited by a ferocious tribe of savages who put all strangers to death, and the stream was full of frightful monsters, some of them large enough to swallow a canoe with all its contents. They also said that in a high cliff of rocks by the side of the river lived a demon, whose roar was so loud as to shake the earth and destroy all canoes passing up or down stream.

These wonderful stories did not frighten the travelers, and after giving the Indians a few presents they continued on their way. Passing up Fox River, and dragging their canoes across the portage, they floated down the Wisconsin. After a few days' journey the river bluffs on either side disappeared, and while viewing the wild scenery around them their canoe entered the broad Mississippi and they found themselves upon the Father of Waters. The voyageurs landed from their canoes, raised a cross on the bank of the river, and sang praises to the Holy Virgin for her guidance and protection thus far on their journey. Father Marquette pronounced a blessing on the river and christened it with the most sacred name of "Immaculate Conception."

After spending a day in fasting and prayers their canoes were again put on the water and they commenced descending the river. While floating down stream they discovered on the east bank, near the present site of the city of Alton, a high cliff of rocks rising in bold relief from the water's edge. This cliff for many years afterward was known as the "Ruined Castle," and is the site of a thrilling legend in Indian tradition. On landing here they beheld a sight which reminded them that the devil was lord of the wilderness. On the surface of rock next to the water was painted, in red, black and green, a pair of monsters, each of them as large as an ox, with horns like an elk, heads like a tiger, and with a frightful expression of countenance. The face of these monsters resembled that of a man, the body covered with scales like a fish, with tails so long as to reach three times around them. These terrible looking monsters (representing Indian gods) so frightened Father Marquette that he fled from the place in terror, and hastened on board of his canoe.

As the travelers were passing down the river, conversing about the hideous painting on the rock, they were suddenly aroused to real danger. Here a torrent of muddy water came rushing across the clear current, boiling and surging, carrying in its course drift-wood, consisting of brush and uprooted trees. Their light bark canoes were whirled about on the dark, angry water, like a twig in a swollen brook, and with great difficulty their frail crafts were kept from swamping in the foaming billows. They had passed the mouth of the Missouri River, and with great rapidity their canoes floated down the swollen stream.

The voyageurs descended the Mississippi River to its junction with the Arkansas, when they became satisfied that the great river emptied into the Gulf of Mexico, instead of the Pacific Ocean, consequently they turned their canoes up stream on their return homeward toward Canada.

THE VOYAGEURS AT LA VANTUM.

On a clear warm day in September, 1673, two bark canoes were seen slowly gliding up the Illinois River, whose placid waters had never before reflected the face of a white man. These canoes were propelled up stream by sails and oars, and as they went forward the voyageurs caused the wild woods along the shore to, resound with songs of praise. On the sail of the foremost canoe was painted various devices, representing a coat-of-arms, a pipe of peace, and a cross, emblematical of power, friendship, and Christianity. The voyageurs were much delighted with the country along the placid stream, and made many comments on the beauty of the surrounding country. Large herds of buffalo were seen feeding on the green meadows, and at the sound of the oars elk, deer and antelope would rise from their lair, and bound away across the distant plains.

Wild geese and swans were swimming in the river, while flocks of paroquets made merry the lonely waters with their songs.

This party of travelers consisted of nine persons, Louis Joliet, Jacques Marquette, five oarsmen, and two Indian interpreters. While forcing their light crafts up stream they were surprised to come suddenly upon a large town on the left bank of the river, while back of it the great meadow was covered with camping-tents, and swarming with human beings. This was the great Illinois town called La Vantum, situated near the present site of Utica, and known in after years as the great landmark of the west.

As the voyageurs approached the town the Indians in great numbers collected on the river bank to see these strange people, never before having looked upon the face of a white man. Warriors armed with war clubs, bows and arrows lined the shore, prepared to give the strangers battle if enemies, or greet them kindly if friends. The canoes came to a halt, when Joliet displayed the "wampum," a token of friendship, at the sight of which the warriors lowered their weapons and motioned the voyageurs to come ashore. Father Marquette, with a pipe of peace in one hand and a small gold cross in the other, approached the Indians, who in astonishment collected around him, offering up mementoes to appease the wrath of the great Manitou, from whom they believed the strangers had come. The tourists left their canoes, being conducted to the lodge of the head chief, Chassagoac, where they were kindly entertained for the night.

On the following day, in the presence of all the chiefs and principal warriors, Joliet took formal possession of the country in the name of Louis XIV, after which Marquette preached to this vast assembly. Under Marquette's preaching many were converted, and baptized in accordance to the Catholic church. Among the converts was Chassagoac, the head chief of the Illinois Indians, who continued in the faith, and in after years was a friend of the early pioneers on the Illinois River. Marquette gave this chief a number of christian mementoes, consisting of crosses, crucifixes, etc., all of which he wore on his person for more than fifty years, and at the time of his death they were buried with him.

On the third day the canoes of the explorers were again on the river, and they continued their journey eastward. On reaching the mouth of the Chicago River Joliet, with three companions, continued on his way to Canada to report to the governor, while Marquette with two others went to Green Bay for the purpose of converting the Indians. As

Joliet was passing down the rapids of the St. Lawrence River, near Montreal, his canoe upset, and his journal, with all other valuables, were lost.

These explorers published no account of their travels, and the world was but little wiser for their journey, except to establishing the fact that the Mississippi River did not flow into the Pacific Ocean, and Illinois was a rich country.

CHAPTER III.

THE CROSS RAISED ON THE BANK OF CHICAGO RIVER.

FATHER MARQUETTE remained at Green Bay only a short time, his health being bad, and the Winnebago Indians, with whom he sojourned, were unwilling to abandon the religion of their fathers for Christianity. It being impressed on the mind of Marquette that his stay on earth would be short, and before departing hence, he felt it his duty to visit the Illinois Indians and again establish among them a mission in honor of the Holy Virgin.

Late in the fall Marquette, accompanied by two of his countrymen, Pierre and Jacques, with two Indians, left Green Bay for the Illinois River. The weather was cold, the wind high, and with great difficulty they coasted along the western shore of Lake Michigan. Frequently the travelers were compelled to land from the turbulent water, draw their canoe on the beach, and wait for the wind and waves to subside. After a long, perilous voyage the travelers reached the mouth of Chicago river, and ascended it about three leagues to a grove of timber. Here Marquette was taken very sick, and winter set in, the river froze up, and the prairie covered with snow and ice. Near the river bank Pierre and Jacques built a hut, covering and siding it with buffalo skins, and here in this rude tenement they lived about three months.

Buffalo and deer were plenty, and the Indians from a neighboring village supplied them with corn, honey and maple sugar, so they did not want for the necessaries of life. For many days Marquette was prostrated by disease so he could not leave his couch, and his friends believed that his time of departure was nigh. Having a great desire to establish a mission among the Illinois Indians before death overtook him, Marquette begged his two companions, Pierre and Jacques, to join him in nine days' devotion to the Virgin, and through her interposition his disease relented and he gained strength daily. Indians from a village two leagues distant frequently visited their hut, and Marquette, feeble as he was, preached to them, and many became converted to Christianity. Near their hut they built a temporary altar, over which was raised a large wooden cross. The converted Indians were instructed, while praying, to look upon this cross and thereby all their sins were remitted.

MISSION OF IMMACULATE CONCEPTION.

The winter was now passed, snow and ice had disappeared from the prairie, and the warm sun of early spring not only animated nature, but it gave strength and vitality to Father Marquette. His cough had almost ceased, his tall, manly form, which had been bent by rheumatism, was now erect, and he sang songs of praise to the Holy Virgin for his restoration to health. After taking an affectionate farewell of the converted Indians Marquette, with his two companions in a bark canoe, left for the great Illinois town.

With sail and oars the voyageurs urged their canoe down the Des Plaines and Illinois Rivers, while the surrounding woods reëchoed their songs of praise. Birds were singing among the trees, squirrels chirping in the groves, while elk and deer bounded away at the sound of the approaching canoe. Swans, pelicans and wild geese would rise from the water and fly squawking down stream, while beaver and otter were sporting in the water and diving under their canoe. Far and near the prairie was covered with herds of buffalo, some basking in the sun, while others were feeding on the early spring grass.

When Marquette arrived at La Vantum the Indians received him as though he was an angel from heaven, some of whom fell on their knees before him, asking forgiveness for past sins. Chassagone, the head chief, whom Marquette had baptized the year before, was so delighted at meeting the holy father that he embraced him, and wept for joy. On the following day after Marquette's arrival all the Indians, old and young, assembled on the meadow above the town to hear good tidings from the great French Manitou, the name given to Christ. Around him were seated on the ground five hundred chiefs and old warriors, behind them stood one thousand five hundred young braves, while around these were collected all the squaws and papooses of the town. Marquette, standing in the midst of this vast assembly, displayed to them two pictures, painted on canvas, one of the Virgin, and the other of Christ, telling them of God, of heaven, of hell, and of a judgment to come, when all the Indians clapped their hands and shouted for joy. By Marquette's direction the Indians tore down the temple and images erected to the god of war, and built a chapel on its site. When the chapel was completed all the chiefs and old warriors assembled therein, when Marquette dedicated it in honor of the Holy Virgin, giving it the same name which he had already given to the Mississippi River, "The Immaculate Conception."

Each day the chapel was filled with converts, and Marquette preached to them, baptizing old and young; a large number of converts were enrolled in the church book, and saved from perdition. On Easter Sunday the chapel was decorated with flowers and evergreens, representing crosses, anchors, crucifixes, etc. Incense was burned on the altar, and lights were kept burning during the day, according to the custom of the Catholic church. This day was a joyous one, and long remembered by the Indians, but with it ended the ministry of Marquette among the redmen of the west.

Spring had now come, the groves were once more green, and the prairies again covered with grass and flowers, but it did not bring health and vigor to the failing priest. His disease had again returned in its worst form, and he felt that his life was fast passing away. After spending two days and nights in prayer, communing with Christ and the Holy Virgin, he concluded to return to Canada, where he could receive the sacrament from the hands of his brethren before he died.

On the third day after Easter the natives were assembled in the chapel, when Marquette, pale and feeble as he was, preached to them, instructing his converts in the ways of Christianity, telling them that he was about to depart for Canada, but promised to send a priest to teach them in the ways of salvation. The Indians heard the news in sadness, gathering around the holy father and begging him to remain with them. But he told his brethren that his work was ended, that a few weeks would close his pilgrimage here on earth, and before departing hence he desired to return to Canada and leave his bones among his countrymen.

Marquette's canoe was once more put on the water, and with his two faithful companions he commenced his journey eastward. About five hundred warriors, some in canoes and others mounted on ponies, accompanied Marquette as far as Lake Michigan, and there received from him the parting blessing. After parting with the Indians, Marquette's canoe, with sails hoisted and oars applied, coasted near the shore around the head of the Lake. Pierre and Jacques with all their power plied the oars to increase the speed, while the sick priest lay prostrated in the bottom of the canoe communing with the Virgin and with angels.

DEATH OF MARQUETTE.

On the 19th of May, 1675, while near Sleeping Bear Point, Marquette felt that his time had come, and told his companions to land him on the beach of the lake, so he might receive the sacrament before he died. On a high point of land, at the mouth of a small stream which still bears his name, they built a bark hut, and carried thither the dying priest. With his eyes fixed on a crucifix which one of his companions held before him, and while murmuring the name of Mary and Jesus, he breathed his last. His companions dug a grave on the bank of the stream near the place where he died, and buried him there. In obedience to his request they erected over his grave a cross made of bass-wood timber, on which were engraved his name and date of his death. After burying Marquette Pierre and Jacques again put their canoe on the water and continued their journey toward Canada, conveying thither the sad news of his death. Three years after Marquette's death a party of Indians from Point St. Ignace, who were converted under Marquette's preaching some years before, went to Lake Michigan, opened the grave, and took up the remains. After scraping off the putrid flesh, washing and drying the bones, they were placed in a box made of birch-bark and carried home with them. With the remains of the holy father they turned their canoe homeward, singing and chanting praises as they went on their way. Seven miles above Point St. Ignace they were met by a large delegation of Indians in canoes, who formed a procession to escort the remains to the mission.

With their faces blacked, oars muffled, and singing a funeral dirge, the procession slowly approached the mission, and were met at the landing by priest-traders and Indians, all of whom wore badges of mourning. With a solemn ceremony the remains of Father Marquette were received at the mission, and buried beneath the altar of the little chapel of St. Ignace which he had built some years before.

Two centuries have now passed away since the burial of Marquette, and long since the little chapel of St. Ignace has disappeared, but the spot where it stood was hallowed by the French and converted Indians, and continues to be pointed out to strangers visiting the place.

For many years after the death of Marquette the French sailors on the lakes kept his picture nailed to the mast-head as a guardian angel, and when overtaken by storm and perils at sea they would pray to the holy father beseeching him to calm the winds and still the troubled waters in order that they might reach port in safety.

RESURRECTING MARQUETTE'S BONES.

The old chapel of St. Ignace continued to stand guard over the remains of Marquette until the year 1706, when it was burned down and the mission removed to the island of Mackinaw. For many years after the mission was removed from this old historic place religious enthusiasts were in the habit of visiting Point St. Ignace, and offering up prayers on this sacred spot. For ages the place where the chapel stood was hallowed by zealous Catholics, but no steps were taken to memorize the grave or recover the bones of the great missionary and explorer, until a few years ago this matter was brought to public notice. In the spring of 1877 Father Jocker, the village priest, began to agitate the subject of resurrecting the bones of Marquette, and everywhere it met with public favor. A time having been set for that purpose, people from a distance collected at Point St. Ignace, and amid a large assembly of enthusiastic persons the remains were exhumed.

Excavations having been made on the site of the old chapel the relics of the altar of the Holy Virgin were found and taken out. Beneath the altar, in a vault walled with red cedar, was found a large piece of birch-bark in a good state of preservation, and here too were found the remains of Marquette, where they had lain for over two hundred years. The bones, much decayed, some of them mouldered into dust when exposed to the air, were taken out in the presence of a large collection of people, and with proper ceremony buried in a cemetery near by, over which a monument to his memory has been erected.

CHAPTER IV.

LA VANTUM, OR GREAT ILLINOIS TOWN.

THE name of La Vantum was applied to the great Illinois town over a century ago by the French and half-breeds at Peoria. The name in the Indian language is said to mean a great place, a large town, capital for a tribe, etc. In letters written by Jesuits and early explorers of the west it is spoken of as the great town of Illinois, where chiefs and warriors from other villages met for council. Joliet called this place Kaskaskia, but by La Salle and subsequent explorers it is spoken of as the great Illinois town. The number of its inhabitants has been variously estimated by different explorers, ranging from five to eight thousand. Marquette said he found here five hundred chiefs and old warriors, and fifteen hundred young braves. Seven years afterward Father Hennepin counted four hundred and sixty-eight lodges, each of which contained from two to four families. Others speak of it as a large town, occupying the river bank for a mile or more in length, and extending back some distance on the prairie.

This great Indian town of the west has long since disappeared, and like many of the ancient cities of the Old World both history and tradition fail to point out its exact location. Some antiquarians have located it near Buffalo Rock, others at the mouth of Little Vermillion, as many Indian relics are found at each of these places. But in comparing the different accounts given of this town, from its first discovery by Joliet to its final distruction by the allied forces, a period of nearly one hundred years, it is shown conclusively to have stood on or near the site of old Utica, and here relics of it are found in great quantities. History says it was on the north bank ot the river, in plain view of Fort St. Louis, and the French passed to and from it in their canoes.

On the north side of the river is a large bottom prairie, extending from Buffalo Rock to the Little Vermillion, about nine miles long and one and a half miles in width. Near the middle of this prairie, below the foot of the rapids, the river is confined to a deep, narrow channel, and the bank rises gradually from the water's edge until it reaches high land in the rear, forming a sloping plateau, elevated above the floods of the Illinois, and for beauty of location is scarcely surpassed by any place on the river. In early times this point was considered the head of navigation, and consequently it would be the termination of the Illinois and Michigan canal. In 1834 a town was laid off here by Simon Crozier, and people prophesied that it was destined to be a large city. Steamboats at St. Louis put out their sign for Utica, and travelers for the Lake country or eastward bound landed here, thence by stage to Chicago. Corn now grows on this town site. Two or three old dilapidated, unoccupied buildings only remain of this once great paper city, and Utica, like its predecessor, La Vantum, exists only in history of the past.

Felix La Pance, a French trader at Peoria, frequently visited this town, it being on his route to and from Canada, and from 1751 to 1768 traded with the inhabitants, taking their furs on his annual trips east, and paying for them in goods on his return. Some account of this town is found among his papers, now in the possession of his descendants. This account speaks of a town containing five or six hundred lodges standing along the river bank, while back of these, on the prairie, were many camping-tents, occupied by Indians part of the year. On the river bank, near the middle of the town, stood their great council house, surrounded by stockades and various kinds of temporary fortifications. The town was shaded by a few outspreading oaks, and in the midst of them, and close to the river bank, was a large spring of cold water. This spring, spoken of by La Pance, cannot be found on the old town site, but whoever will take the trouble to examine the river at this point when low will observe a short distance from shore the bubbles from a spring under water. Waba, an Indian chief of some note, who lived at a village on the south side of the river, opposite Lake Depue, in speaking of this town said, in his youthful days there was a large spring of cold water here by the side of the trail, but afterward it sank and came out under the river as we now see it.

A short distance from the river is a range of gravelly knolls, where the Indians had their caches or subterranean store-house for depositing corn. The remains of these caches were plain to be seen in the early settlement of the country, and in some places these relics still exist, notwithstanding they have been plowed over for many years. Back of the town, on high prairie, was their burying-ground, where the ashes of posterity mingled with those of their ancestors for many generations. Many small mounds were found here in the early settlement of the country, but have been mostly leveled down in searching for treasures. These mounds are supposed to have been raised over the remains of chiefs and great warriors, and are said to have contained some of the valuables of the deceased. About sixty years ago, Waba, the Indian chief above referred to, took from one of these mounds many trinkets, among which was a silver medallion head of Louis XIV, bearing date 1670, being three years before Marquette's first visit to this place, and in all probability it was given to a convert by that missionary.

I am informed by James Clark, the owner of the land around old Utica, and also by one of his tenants, that every year many Indian relics are plowed up. These relics consist of human teeth and fragments of small bones, with flint arrow-heads, stone hatchets, and various kinds of trinkets.

THE GREAT WESTERN EXPLORER.

Seven years after Joliet and Marquette discovered the Upper Mississippi, La Salle obtained a patent from the King of France authorizing him to explore and take possession in the king's name all the country west of the great lakes. La Salle's success and failure in this great enterprise is a matter of history, and much of it foreign to our purpose. but as he was identified with the early settlement of Illinois a few facts relating to him may interest the reader.

Robert Cavalier (La Salle being only a title) was born in the city of Rouen, France, in the year 1643, of wealthy parents, and educated for the priesthood.

In person he is said to have been large and muscular, of an iron constitution, possessing a fine intellect, and well qualified for the enterprise in which he embarked. He inherited from his ancestors a large fortune, which was used in advancing his enterprise, but squandered in consequence of misplaced confidence in those with whom he associated. Although La Salle made his mark in history, his life was one of hardship, exposure and deprivations, and he finally died by the hand of an assassin in the wilds of Texas.

A few years ago, while strolling through the city of Rouen, my guide pointed out an old palace standing on high ground, and overlooking the river Seine. For beauty of architecture and antique appearance this palace has no equal in the old Norman capital. This old palace, said my guide, was once the residence of the Duke of Normandy, better known as William the Conqueror, and from its portico this great warrior addressed his lords and nobles on the day he left Normandy for the conquest of England. In this palace, continued my guide, now lives Count Cavalier, a descendant of the family of La Salle, and near by, in an antique looking house, is pointed out as the birth-place of the great explorer, and is now occupied by a descendant of his family.

LA SALLE AND FRIENDS WESTERN BOUND.

In the summer of 1679 La Salle built a vessel at the head of Niagara River for the purpose of navigating the Upper Lakes. This vessel was of sixty tons burden, carrying lateen sails, and called the Griffin. It was armed with a number of small cannon, and a large wooden eagle surmounted its prow, while the monster for which it was named, according to Grecian mythology, was painted on its canvas. In La Salle's party was an Italian officer, second in command, named Tonti, also three Jesuit priests, Hennepin, Gabriel and Zenche, the former known by his surname, and the two latter by their given names only.

All things being ready the cannons fired a salute, the sails spread to the breeze, and the Griffin moved forward, plowing through the maiden waves of Lake Erie. After many days' sail the vessel passed through a small lake, which La Salle gave the name of St. Clair, in honor of that saint, whose name appeared that day in the calendar. After a voyage of four weeks the Griffin arrived at Mackinaw, and was safely moored in its harbor. The goods brought by the Griffin were exchanged for furs at a large profit, and the vessel loaded with pelts and furs started back for Niagara, but was never heard of afterward.

Late in November, La Salle, accompanied by fourteen persons, left Mackinaw in four canoes and coasted along the eastern shore of Lake Michigan. They carried with them a blacksmith's forge, carpenter tools, and other utensils required in building a fort, besides a large amount of merchandise to trade with the Indians. On the second day out they were overtaken by a storm, which compelled them to land, drag their canoes on the beach, where they remained four days waiting for the waves to subside. Again trusting their frail barks to the waters of the lake, they were overtaken on the following day by a severe gale, and amid the lashing of waves their canoes drifted on a barren, rocky island some distance from the main-land. Here they remained two days without shelter or fire, while their blankets alone protected them from the cold winter blasts. At last the voyageurs reached the mouth of St. Joseph River, and remained here some days waiting for Tonti and his thirty-five companions, who came through the wilderness of Michigan. In bark canoes La Salle and his command commenced ascending St. Joseph River, crossing the portage and down the Kankakee to its junction with the Des Plaines.

It was midwinter when the travelers reached La Vantum, the great Illinois town, and they found it deserted, the inhabitants having gone off on the winter hunt, according to their custom. Being in a starving condition, La Salle ordered one of the caches opened, and they took therefrom twenty minots of corn, hoping at some future time to compensate the Indians for this robbery. After spending two days in desolated lodges of the town the party again boarded their canoes and continued on their way down the river. About five leagues below La Vantum, at the mouth of a stream supposed to have been Bureau Creek, the voyageurs landed and sent out their hunters in search of buffalo. The following day being New Year, 1680, it was agreed to spend it in camp, saying mass and taking the sacrament in accordance to an old custom in the Catholic church. Before leaving Canada Father Hennepin provided himself with a miniature altar, which folded up like an army chair and could be carried on the back the same as a knapsack. With this altar on his back Father Hennepin started off through the woods in search of a suitable place for worship, followed by the other priests and the rest of the party. A place was selected, a cross raised, the altar erected, and the holy father preached to his companions, causing the wild woods to resound with exhortations and songs of praise. After preaching and saying mass the sacred emblems were placed by the side of the altar, preparatory to taking the sacrament. But great was

Father Hennepin's astonishment to find the wine vessel empty, as one of the party, a blacksmith by trade, nicknamed La Forge, had drank it up while on the road. For this act of sacrilege Father Hennepin pronounced against him a curse equal to the one the Pope pronounced against Martin Luther.

FRENCH AT PEORIA LAKE.

According to history, on the 3d of January, 1680, the inhabitants of an Indian village situated on the west bank of Peoria Lake were surprised to see eight canoes filled with armed men opposite their town. These canoes were all abreast, presenting a formidable appearance, and the men seated in them held guns in their hands ready for an attack or defense. The canoes rounded to and landed at the village, causing a great panic among the Indians, some of whom fled in terror, while others seized their arms and were prepared to defend themselves. Amid the confusion that followed La Salle sprang ashore and presented to the astonished natives the calumet (a token of friendship), while Father Hennepin caught several frightened papooses and soothed their fears with kindness and small presents.

The French pitched their tents in the Indian village and remained there for some days; but discontentment among the men, and fearing treachery of the Indians, caused La Salle to remove to a place of greater security. A site to build a fort was selected and all the valuables at the camp transferred thereto. On account of the gloomy prospect, the discontentment and desertion of some of the men, La Salle named this fort Creve Cœur, which in English is Broken Heart.

FORT CREVE CŒUR.

Father Hennepin, in his journal, says in January, 1680, he went with La Salle down the river in search of a suitable place to build a fort. An eminence on the south side of the river being selected, which was defended on two sides by ravines cut deep by rains, and on one side by a steep bank, so the site was accessible from only one way. A ditch was dug on the land side connecting the two ravines, and the site inclosed by palisades. The soldiers were lodged in huts within this inclosure, and two cabins built, one for La Salle and Tonti, and the other for the three friars.

Much has been written about the site of Fort Creve Cœur, but the only place in this vicinity answering the above description is at the village of Wesley, which is located on the east side of the river, three miles below Peoria, and this is generally conceded to have been the site of the old fort.

Father Hennepin lamented the loss of wine, which

prevented him from administering the sacrament, but each morning and evening all the occupants of the fort were summoned to his cabin for prayers. Fathers Gabriel and Zenobe spent most of their time in the Indian village, preaching and instructing the natives in the ways of Christianity, but they made but few proselytes.

About the 1st of February Father Hennepin, in a canoe, accompanied by two of his countrymen, left the fort on a voyage of discovery; passing down the Illinois River to its mouth, they ascended the Mississippi to the Falls of St. Anthony; here Hennepin and his comrades were made prisoners by the Indians, and remained in confinement for several months, but afterward they were liberated and returned to Canada. On arriving at Montreal Father Hennepin sailed for France, and published a book of his adventures in the new world.

CHAPTER V.

LA SALLE IN AN INDIAN CAMP.

WAR having existed for a long time between the Illinois and Iroquois Indians, La Salle had now to use his influence to make peace between the contending parties, as this hostility would endanger his enterprise. The Illinois Indians regarded this interference on the part of La Salle as treachery to them, and in council they had decided to put him and his comrades to death. On learning of this decision of the Indians, La Salle formed and executed a bold and hazardous project, of going alone, unarmed, to the Indian camp, for the purpose of vindicating his conduct. His bravery and eloquence astonished the natives, and completely changed their purposes. The calumet was smoked, presents exchanged, and a treaty of amity concluded between the French and Indians.

In March, La Salle, accompanied by two of his countrymen, returned to Canada to obtain supplies, as he was now convinced that the Griffin, with her cargo, had been lost. While they were forcing their canoe up the rapid current they noticed on the south bank a remarkable cliff of rocks rising from the water's edge and towering above the forest trees. Landing from their canoe they ascended this rock and found it to be a natural fortress, where but little labor would be required to make it impregnable, so that a few soldiers could hold it against a host of savages. When La Salle arrived at Mackinaw he sent word back to Tonti to fortify this rock and make it his stronghold. Although circumstances prevented Tonti from obeying the orders of his superior, nevertheless a fort was built here two years afterward, and around it clustered the first colony in the Mississippi Valley.

When La Salle left for Canada Tonti took command of the fort, which he was expected to hold until the return of his superior. Mutiny arose among his command, and a short time after La Salle left, all the soldiers except three deserted and made their way back to Canada. Tonti being left with only three soldiers and two Jesuit priests, abandoned Fort Creve Cœur, and it was never occupied by troops afterward.

HENRI DE TONTI.

Among the many adventurers who accompanied La Salle to America, and took in exploring the wilds of the west, was a young Italian of noble birth by the name of Henri de Tonti. Young Tonti with his father's family were banished from Italy on account of having taken part in a revolution of that country, and they found a home at Rouen, France. Tonti having a military education joined the French army and served five years, part of the time as captain of National Guards. At the close of the war he was discharged from service, came to America with La Salle, and took part in his enterprise. La Salle made Tonti his lieutenant, second in command, and the sequel shows that he was worthy of the trust placed in him.

Part of Tonti's right hand having been shot off in the Sicilian war its place was supplied by an iron one, which he always kept covered with a glove. With this iron hand Tonti on two different occasions broke the heads, or knocked out the teeth, of disorderly Indians, which caused them to believe that he possessed supernatural power. Tonti brought with him from France a large sum of money, which was used in common with La Salle in exploring and taking possession of the country, and also in trade with the Indians.

The late Dr. Sparks says history never can do ample justice to Tonti, as his life was one of patriotism, self sacrifice, and the discovery and settlement of the Great West belongs mainly to him.

Forty years of Tonti's life was spent in the wilds of the west, enduring hardships, dangers and deprivations, associating with savages, and without the benefits or comforts of civilization. His fortune squandered, his health and manhood sacrificed, stripped of his hard-earned laurels, he became a wanderer along the Gulf of Mexico, but at last returned to die at Fort St. Louis, and his bones now rest on the bank of the Illinois River, at the west end of Starved Rock.

In one of the Louvre picture galleries in Paris can be seen a full length portrait of a youthful looking man, dressed in a French uniform, with epaulets on his shoulders and an eagle on his breast. His left hand holds a sword, while the right one presents a singular appearance, as though deformed, but hidden by a glove. This tall, graceful figure, and the piercing black eyes, never fail to attract the attention of strangers, and inquiry would naturally arise for the history of the person here represented. Below this portrait is painted, in large letters, the name "*Henri de Tonti, la voyageur des Amerique.*"

THE FRENCH AT LA VANTUM.

Soon after the troops deserted their post at Fort Creve Cœur, Tonti, with those remaining, consisting of Fathers Gabriel and Zenobe and three soldiers, abandoned the place. All the valuables in the fort were put into two canoes, when the party ascended the river as far as La Vantum, and here they found quarters among the Indians with the intention of awaiting La Salle's return from Canada. Tonti applied himself in learning the Indian languages, the two priests were engaged in preaching to the Indians, while the soldiers spent the honeymoon with their squaws, whom they had recently married.

About three miles from the town, in the midst of a thick grove of timber, Fathers Gabriel and Zenobe erected a temporary altar, and every third day they repaired thither for prayer and meditation. Here in this lonely spot, far away from the noise and bustle of the town, the two holy friars would spend long summer days from early morning until late at night communing with the Virgin, and with saints and angels. Notwithstanding these priests preached and prayed with the Indians almost daily, promising them great success in war, hunting, etc., if they would embrace the Christian religion, but few converts were made. Chassagoac, the head chief, having been converted several years before under the preaching of Marquette, still continued in the faith. This chief with his family and a few of his friends had taken the sacrament from the hands of the priests, but all other chiefs and warriors adhered to the religion of their fathers.

The wine brought from Canada for sacramental purposes having been drank by La Forge, as previously stated, it became necessary to procure a substitute, as the administration of the sacred rites could not be dispensed with. During the winter the priests gathered a quantity of wild grapes, pressed out the juice, and put away in the sacramental cask for future use. This wine answered the purpose very well so long as the weather remained cool, but during the summer it soured and became unfit for use. When the time came to administer the sacrament Tonti, the three soldiers with their wives, Chassagoac and family, with a few of his friends, were assembled in the council-house on the Sabbath day to receive the sacred emblems. Father Gabriel, wrapped in his long black robe, with a gold cross suspended from his neck, preached to them, telling them of Christ, of the Virgin, of the apostles, saints, and of the kingdom to come. After preaching all knelt around the altar, engaged in prayer, while Father Gabriel made preparations to administer the sacrament, but was horrified to find the wine sour, and the miracle of transubstantiation, that is, converting the wine into the real blood of Christ, could not be performed, consequently the sacramental service for the present had to be dispensed with.

Time hung heavy with the French, days and weeks passed away, spring was gone, the summer almost ended, and still no news from La Salle. In an Indian village, where there is neither hunting, war parties to fit out, nor national festivals to keep up an excitement, it has a dull, monotonous appearance. Warriors lay under shade-trees sleeping, or amusing themselves in games of chance, while squaws were at work in cornfields, or preparing food for their families. Naked papooses were playing on the green or rolling in the dirt, while young maidens with their lovers were gathering flowers in the grove, fishing on the river bank, or rowing their canoes across its waters, unconscious of the great calamity that was about to befall them.

RECEPTION OF EVIL TIDINGS.

It was near the close of a warm day in the latter part of the summer when a scout arrived with his pony in a foam of sweat, shouting at the top of his voice that the Iroquois were marching against the town. All was now excitement and confusion, squaws screamed, papooses quit their plays on the green and ran away to their homes, warriors caught their weapons, and preparations for defense. The warriors greased their bodies, painted their faces, and ornamented their heads with turkey feathers, and spent the night in singing and dancing. Morning at last came, and with it came the savage Iroquois armed with rifles and other implements of warfare. On receiving notice of the approaching enemy a crowd of excited savages collected around Tonti and his three companions, whom they had previously suspected of treachery, and charged them with being in league with the Iroquois. A report having reached them that a number of Jesuit priests and La Salle himself were with the enemy leading them on to the town. The enraged warriors seized the blacksmith forge tools, with all the goods belonging to the French, and threw them into the river. One of the warriors caught Tonti by the hair of the head, and raised his tomahawk to split open his skull, but a friendly chief caught the savage by the arm, and thereby his life was spared. Tonti, with boldness and self possession which was characteristic of him, defended himself against these charges, and in order to convince them of his good faith offered to accompany them to battle.

Fathers Gabriel and Zenobe at the time of the alarm were away at their altar spending the day in prayer and meditation, and had no warning of the danger that awaited them. On their return home late at night they were surprised to find the town in a whirlpool of excitement, squaws crying, bewailing their fate, warriors dancing, yelling, brandishing their war-clubs to keep up their courage, and offering up sacrifices to the Manitou of battle. On the arrival of the two priests the savages charged them with treachery, and of being the cause of the Iroquois invading their country. The priests with uplifted hands called God to witness their innocence of the charge, but their denial did not change the minds of the excited Indians. A loud clamor was raised for their blood, when a number of warriors sprang forward with uplifted tomahawks to slay them, but as they drew nigh and about to strike the fatal blow Father Gabriel drew from his bosom a small gold image of the Holy Virgin, and held it before the faces of the would-be murderers. On seeing this sacred talisman in the hands of the priest the executioners paused a moment, and then returned their tomahawks to their belts. Father Zenobe in after years said this was only one of the many instances of the Holy Virgin protecting the Jesuits of North America.

During the night all the squaws and papooses, with the aged warriors unable to bear arms, were placed in canoes and taken down the river about three leagues, to a large, marshy island. About sixty warriors were left here for their protection, and all of them secreted themselves among the reeds and high grass, but the sequel shows their hiding place was discovered by the enemy, and this place of supposed safety became their tomb.

BATTLE AND MASSACRE.

At the time of the Iroquois invasion there were only about five hundred warriors in La Vantum, the head chief, Chassagoac, and a portion of his braves having gone to a distant village for the purpose of attending a religious feast. But this band, small as it was, boldly crossed the river at daylight and met the enemy, whose number was five times their own. While they were ascending the bluff a scout met them saying the enemy were crossing the prairie close at hand, and as the invaders approached the river timber they were surprised to meet the Illinoisans who were lying in ambush, and received them with a deadly fire. At this unexpected attack the Iroquois were panic-stricken, and fled from the field, leaving the ground covered with their dead and wounded. But they soon rallied and the fight became bloody, arrows and rifle balls flying thick and fast, while the woods far and near resounded with the wild whoops of contending savages. In the midst of the fight Tonti undertook the perilous task of mediating between the contending parties. Laying aside his gun, and taking a wampum belt in his hand, holding it above his head as a flag of truce, and amid showers of arrows and rifle balls, he walked boldly forward to meet the enemy. As he approached the Iroquois warriors collected around him in a threatening manner, one of whom attempted to stab him to the heart, but the knife striking a rib made only a long, shallow gash. As the savage was about to repeat the blow, a chief came up, and seeing the victim was a white man, protected him from further assaults, and applied a bandage to the wound to stop the bleeding. The fighting having ceased, a warrior took Tonti's hat, and placing it on the muzzle of his gun started toward the Illinoisans, who on seeing it supposed the owner was killed, and again renewed the fight. While the battle was raging a warrior reported that three French men, armed with guns, were with the Illinoisans and firing on them. On making this announcement the Iroquois warriors became enraged at Tonti, and again gathered around him, some for killing and others for protection. One of the warriors caught him by the hair of his head, raising it up, and with his long knife was about to take off his scalp, when Tonti, with his iron hand, knocked down his assailant. Others attacked Tonti with knives and tomahawks, but he was again rescued from death by the principal war chief. For a long time the battle raged with fearful strife, many of the combatants on both sides being slain, but at last the Illinoisans were overpowered and driven from the field. The vanquished fled to their town with the intention of defending it or perish in the attempt.

On the river bank, near the center of the town, stood their great council-house, surrounded by earthworks and stockades, forming a kind of fortification. To this place the remnant of the warriors fled, and in great haste tore down some of the lodges and used the material in strengthening their works of defense.

The Illinoisans had crossed the river in canoes, but their pursuers, having no means of crossing at this point, were obliged to go up the river to the rapids to ford it. In a short time the enemy attacked the town, setting fire to lodges and fortifications, which were soon a mass of flames. Many of the besieged were burned, others slain or made prisoners as they escaped from the flames, and only a few succeeded in making their escape.

When the victory was completed the conquerors bound the prisoners hand and foot, and commenced torturing them to make them reveal the hiding place of the squaws and papooses, and on obtaining the necessary information a party of warriors went in search of them. While these defenseless beings were secreted among the reeds and sage grass of the island, they were discovered by the savage Iroquois, and all of them slain. The sixty warriors left as guards fled on approach of the enemy, and some of them succeeded in making their escape.

CHAPTER VI.

TORTURING PRISONERS.

ON the following day after the battle the victors made preparations to torture the prisoners, and their acts of barbarity probably have never been equaled by any other savages of the west. The warriors were formed into a large circle, and the prisoners, bound hand and foot, conveyed thither; when the work of torture commenced the doomed victims were seated on the ground awaiting their fate, some of whom were weeping or praying, others engaged in singing their death song. The executioner, with his long knife, cut off the nose and ears and pieces of flesh from the body while the prisoners sat writhing with agony, and the ground around them red with human gore. This work of torture continued for some time, limbs and pieces of flesh were cut from different parts of the body, and in some cases the bowels were taken out and trailed on the ground, while the groans and screams of the victims in their agonies of death were terrible to witness. Tonti and his companions looked on in horror at these barbarous acts of the Iroquois, but dare not remonstrate, as they, too, were prisoners, and did not know but a like fate awaited them.

While the torture was going on the two priests were engaged in baptising the victims in order to absolve them from past sins, and as each one was about to expire they held the crucifix before his eyes so he might look on it while giving up the ghost, and through its divine efficacy his soul would be saved from perdition.

When the prisoners were all dead the warriors cut out their hearts, roasted and ate them so as to make them brave.

For a number of days the Iroquois continued to rejoice over their victory, spending the time in singing and dancing around the scalps, causing the timbers and surrounding bluff to re-echo with their wild whoops and yells.

DEATH OF FATHER GABRIEL.

Two days after the Iroquois' victory, the French were set at liberty, and they departed eastward in an old leaky canoe. After going about six leagues, they stopped at the mouth of a creek to repair the canoe and dry their clothing; while thus engaged, Father Gabriel, who was always fond of solitude, wandered off among the thick timber for the purpose of prayer and meditation. When the canoe was repaired, clothes dried, and the time of departure came, Father Gabriel being absent search was made for him, but he could not be found. During the night fires were kept burning along the river bank, and guns discharged to direct him to camp, but all in vain. During the following day they searched the woods far and near for the missing priest, but all to no purpose, so they gave him up for lost, and continued on their journey. For days they mourned the loss of the holy father, as he was an old man of nearly three score and ten, and much devoted to the interest of the church.

It was afterward ascertained that Father Gabriel was taken prisoner by Indians, carried off to their camp to be executed, and while his friends were searching for him these savages were dancing around his scalp. While Father Gabriel was at prayer in the thick timber two Indians approached him in a threatening manner, and with his head uncovered he arose to meet them. In vain he told the savages that he was their friend, having come from afar across the big waters to teach them in the ways of truth and happiness; but regardless of his entreaties, they bound his hands behind his back and led him off a prisoner to their camp. A council was held over the captive, and it was decided that he should die. A stake was driven into the ground, and Father Gabriel, with his hands and feet pinioned, tied to it. Here he sat on the ground, bound to the stake, with his long hair and flowing beard, whitened with the snows of seventy winters, waving to and fro in the wind. The Indians formed a circle around their victim, singing and dancing, and under repeated blows of the war-club he fell to the ground and expired. Thus perished Father Gabriel, the only heir of a wealthy Burgundian house, who had given up a life of ease and comfort in the old world to preach the gospel to the heathens of the west, and who, at last, became his murderers.

Four years after the tragedy above narrated a trader at Fort St. Louis bought of an Indian a small gold image of the Virgin Mary, with Father Gabriel's name engraved thereon. This image had been presented to the holy father by the bishop of Normandy, on the day he sailed for America, and he had carried it in his bosom near his heart until the day of his death. Many years after the recovery of this golden image it was carried back to France, and is now to be seen in the museum of Rouen.

A SCENE OF HORROR.

It was midwinter, three months after the massacre of the Illinois Indians, when La Salle with twelve companions returned from Canada to look after his little colony on the Illinois River. As the canoes passed rapidly down the swollen stream the eyes of the travelers were directed to Starved Rock, where they expected to find Tonti within his fortification. But no palisades were there; no smoke ascended from its summit, nor signs of human habitation could be seen. Passing down the rapid current a mile and a half, the travelers were surprised to find the great town of the west had disappeared. The large meadow formerly covered with lodges and camping-tents, and swarming with human beings, was now a lonely waste, a fit representative of death and desolation. On the charred poles which had formed the framework of lodges were many human heads partly robbed of flesh by birds of prey. Packs of wolves fled at their approach, and flocks of buzzards raised from their hideous repast and flew squawking away to distant trees. Even the burying-grounds showed marks of the vindictive malice of the victors having made war on the dead as well as the living. Graves had been opened and bones taken out and piled up in heaps, or broken into fragments and scattered about over the prairie. The scaffold containing the dead had been torn down and their contents thrown hither and thither on the meadow. Everywhere the ground was strewn with mangled bodies and broken bones of the unfortunate Illinoisans.

In the midst of the ruins the conquerors had erected an altar to the god of war, and the poles surrounding it were capped with heads of victims, whose long hair and ghastly features were sickening to look on. The stench arising from putrefaction was so offensive, and the scene so horrifying, that La Salle and his party turned away from it and encamped for the night on the opposite side of the river. During the long winter night the loneliness was made intolerable by the howling of wolves, and buzzards winging their way back and forth through the dark domain.

On the following morning La Salle returned to the ancient town and examined the skulls of many of the victims to see if he could find among them the remains of Tonti and his party, but they all appeared to have been the heads of Indians. On the bank of the river were planted six posts painted red, and on each of these was a figure of a man drawn in white. La Salle believed these figures represented six white men, prisoners in the hands of the Indians, it being the number of Tonti's party.

La Salle and his comrades again boarded their canoes and started down the river, hoping to learn something in relation to the fate of their countrymen, but nothing was discovered. As the travelers passed down the river they saw on the island where the squaws and papooses had taken refuge many human figures standing erect but motionless. With great caution they landed from their canoes to examine these figures, and found them to be partly consumed bodies of squaws who had been bound to a stake and then burned. Fires had been made at their feet, consuming the flesh off their legs and crisping their bodies, but leaving the remains bound to the stake, standing erect as though in life. Poles were stuck into the marsh and papooses placed thereon, while others were hanging by the neck from limbs of trees, with the flesh partly eaten off their bodies by birds of prey. The sight of these dead bodies was so revolting to look upon that the French turned away from them in horror, and continued on their way down the river.

STARVED ROCK.

This remarkable rock is so closely identified with the early history of the Illinois country, and so often referred to in our story, the reader will pardon me for this digression from the narrative in describing it.

On the south bank of the Illinois River, eight miles below Ottawa, and near the foot of the rapids, is a remarkable cliff known as Starved Rock. This rocky cliff rises almost perpendicularly from the water's edge to the height of one hundred and thirty-six feet, and is separated from neighboring cliffs by a wide chasm, which shows signs of having been produced by some convulsion of nature. Three sides of this rock rise like a watch-tower, but the fourth side, next to the bluff, recedes inward, and at one place can be ascended by a steep, rocky pathway. The walls of this cliff consist of grey sandstone, partly hid by forest trees, and when viewed from a distance has the appearance of an old castle of feudal times.

Starved Rock is of a circular form, and in viewing it from every standpoint it has a bold, majestic appearance. On the north side, next to the river, the cliff is perpendicular, rising in towering masses, one rock upon the other, and overlooking the rapid stream which flows at its base. In some places the walls of this cliff are smooth, and thick layers of rock look like the work of art, while at other places they are rough with overhanging crags, under which are many dark, dismal looking caverns, at one time the abode of wild animals. Out of the many crevices in the rocks stunted cedars grow, and under their branches can be seen patches of cactus and mountain ivy.

The summit of Starved Rock contains about three-fourths of an acre, some of it smooth sandstone, on which are engraved many names of visitors; but the larger portion is covered by earth, with grass and small evergreen trees growing thereon. Here, by the river side, stands this high, isolated rock, the same as it stood centuries ago, overlooking the broad plain below and the many wood-clad islands which divide the swift current of the Illinois River, and here it will continue to stand, a monument of past ages and the admiration of the present. Its bold, towering walls, its high, majestic summit, and its isolated position, make it the most picturesque object on the Illinois River, and for historic reminiscences it is without a parallel in the western country.

The view from the summit of Starved Rock is very fine, and will remind a person of a grand landscape painting or a beautiful panorama. To the north and west is a large bottom prairie, bounded on each side by bluffs covered with forest trees. Through this great meadow flows the Illinois River, which can be seen many miles distant winding about in its serpentine course. On looking down into the river at the base of the rock catfish and turtles can be seen sporting over the sand and rocks in the clear, shallow stream, while shoals of pike and red horse ascend the swift current.

By the early French explorers Starved Rock, known as Le Rocher, has figured extensively in the early history of western discoveries. Two centuries ago La Salle built a fort on its summit, the relics of which are still to be seen, and around this fort was clustered the first colony in the Mississippi Valley. The summit of this rock was at one time the abode of gay and joyous French, where balls, gay parties and wine suppers were held, and here, too, was heard, morning and evening, the songs of praise from the lips of devout Jesuit priests. At another time it was a scene of strife, carnage and desolation, stained with human blood and covered with the bodies of the slain. Of late years pleasure parties have frequent dances on this rock; but they do not consider that here was once the dance of death, where the infant, the mother, the young maiden, the brave warrior and aged chief suffered and died, and their bones. bleached white by rain and sun, could be seen for many years afterward.

Two hundred years has made but little change in the appearance of Starved Rock. The same fort-like walls remain, and probably the same stunted cedars. crown its summit; but the surroundings have undergone a great change. The great meadow which it overlooks, once covered with grass and wild flowers, and sometimes blackened with herds of buffalo, is now occupied by farms in close succession. To the north, across the wide bottom prairie, is seen the village of Utica, with its cement mills and warehouses, by the side of which pass the canal and railroad. To the west, five miles below but in plain view, are the flourishing cities of Peru and La Salle, with their church steeples glittering in the sunbeams. Steam and canal boats are seen in the river, and trains of cars passing and repassing on the different railroads. Evidences of agriculture, commerce and civilization are now seen from the summit of this rock, and the familiar peals of church and school bells are heard, instead ot the wild war-whoop of savages while engaged in a bloody strife, leaving the great meadow below strewn with the dead, as in former times.

CHAPTER VII.

BUILDING OF FORT ST. LOUIS.

LA SALLE met Tonti and his comrades at Mackinaw, and with them descended the Mississippi to its mouth, after which they returned to build a fort on the Illinois River. In the fall of 1682 La Salle, with about forty soldiers under his command, built a fort on the summit of Starved Rock. The place of ascending this rock was improved by breaking off projecting crags and cutting steps in the steep, rocky pathway. The stunted cedars that crowned the summit were cut away to make room for fortifications, and the margin of the rock for about two-thirds of its circumference was encircled by earthworks. Timbers were cut on the river bottom below, and by hand dragged up the stair-like pathway to build a block-house, store-house and dwelling, also to protect a large portion of the summit of the rock with palisades. They built a platform on the trunk of two leaning cedars which grew on the margin of the cliff, on which a windlass was placed to draw water out of the river to supply the garrison. The two small cannon brought from Canada in a canoe were mounted on the wooden ramparts, and all the arms, stores, etc., belonging to the French, were carried here and placed within the stockades. When the fort was completed, and the French flag swung to the breeze, the cannons fired three salutes in honor of Louis XIV, and all the soldiers shouted *vive le roi*.

The fort was named St Louis or Rock Fort, and in its dedication Father Zenobe called on the Holy Virgin to bless and keep it in the true faith, and protect it from the enemies of the cross.

From the wooden ramparts of Fort St. Louis, which were as high and almost as inaccessible as an eagle's nest, the French could look down on the Indian town below, and also on the great meadow which lay spread out before them like a map. Two years before this meadow was the scene of carnage, a waste of death and desolation, blackened by fire, and strewn with the ghastly remains of the slain in the Iroquois victory. But now it was changed: Indians to the number of six thousand had returned, and the river bank for a mile in extent was covered with lodges. Many of the inhabitants of other villages came here to trade, bringing with them venison, buffalo meat, furs, pelts, etc., to exchange for goods. At one time there were encamped around the fort not less than twenty thousand Indians, who came here to trade and seek protection from their much dreaded enemies, the Iroquois. Emigrants from Canada came here and built cabins near the fort, some of whom married squaws, lived in the village with the Indians, and adopted their dress, habits and customs. The colony was called Louisiana, in honor of the king of France, and according to maps drawn at that time it included all of the Mississippi Valley.

TRADE WITH THE INDIANS.

La Salle being now established within his stockades he turned his attention to trading with the Indians, supplying them with goods, and taking furs in exchange. He claimed dominion over all the country west of the lakes by virtue of his patent, and he divided it out among his friends by giving them permits to trade with the Indians. He authorized Richard Bosley to establish a trading post at Cahokia, and Phillip de Beuro one at Green Bay, but compelled them to pay him a royalty on all goods sold and furs bought.

Indians from different parts of the country came to the fort for the purpose of trade, carrying with them large quantities of furs, which were exchanged for goods at a large profit to the trader. Tomahawks, axes, knives, etc., made of flint, were superseded by those of steel, guns took the place of bows and arrows, and blankets as a wearing apparel the place of heavy buffalo robes. Blankets worth three dollars in Montreal would bring one hundred dollars in furs, and a tomahawk that cost fifty cents sold for twenty dollars among the Indians.

LA SALLE'S SUCCESS, FAILURE AND DEATH.

Two years after Fort St. Louis was built La Salle, leaving Tonti in command, returned to Canada, and from thence sailed for France. Obtaining assistance from the court of France La Salle in the following year, with three ships loaded with emigrants, sailed for the mouth of the Mississippi River, with the intention of establishing a colony there. Being unsuccessful in finding the mouth of the Mississippi he landed in Texas, and while traveling across the country on his way to the colony on the Illinois was assassinated by his own men.

In the summer of 1686 Tonti with forty men, in canoes, descended the river to the Gulf of Mexico in search of La Salle, but found no traces of him. Again in 1669 he made a like tour in search of the remnant of the colony, and for the purpose of finding the bones of the great explorer in order to carry them back with him to Fort St. Louis, but this expedition, like the first one, proved a failure.

Although La Salle was dead his colony on the

Illinois River continued to flourish, and the fur trade became a source of great wealth. For eighteen years this trade was conducted by Tonti and La-Frost, the former living at Fort St. Louis, and the latter in Canada.

FORT ST. LOUIS ATTACKED BY IROQUOIS.

Two years after the building of Fort St. Louis it was attacked by two thousand Iroquois warriors, and by them held in siege six days. At that time Tonti was in command of the fort, which contained only fifty soldiers and one hundred Indian allies, and with this small force he put the besiegers to flight.

On a bright, clear day in the latter part of May the great meadow was green with grass, intermixed with flowers of various hues, the forest trees were in full leaf, and the air made fragrant with blossoms of the wild plum and crab-apple. Birds were singing among the branches of trees, and squirrels chirping in the thick river timber, while at a distance was heard the musical notes of the robin and meadow-lark. In the shade of willows and outspreading elms, along the bank of the river, lay the doe and her fawn, lulled to slumber by the hum of the wild bee and grasshopper. All was quiet at Fort St. Louis, and the occupants were delighted with the beauty of the surrounding scenery. To the west, in plain view, lay the great town of LaVantum, with its hundreds of lodges built along the bank of the river, and around which were passing masses of human beings. On the race-track above the town warriors mounted on ponies were practicing horsemanship, while far in the distance squaws were seen at work in their corn fields or gathering greens for the family meal.

It was Sabbath morning, the fourth after Easter; all the inmates of the fort were dressed in their best apparel and seated under the shade of cedars awaiting religious services. Father Zenobe, dressed in his long black robe, with a large gold cross hanging from his neck, was about to commence services when a lone Indian was seen on the bottom prairie going westward, and urging his pony forward at the top of its speed. Father Zenobe after concluding his sermon was about to administer the sacrament when the sentinel at the gate fired his gun to give an alarm. At this unexpected signal the meeting broke up, and every one ran to his post thinking the fort was about to be attacked. On looking in the direction of the town everything appeared in commotion, warriors mounted on ponies riding back and forth at full gallop, squaws and papooses running hither and thither in wild confusion, drums beating, chiefs yelling in giving command, while the cries and lamentations of the frightened people could be heard even at the fort. Tonti, with three companions, came down from the fort, boarded a canoe, and with all haste proceeded down the river to ascertain the cause of this excitement, when the mystery was explained.

A scout had arrived with the intelligence that a large body of Iroquois were only ten leagues distant, and marching on the town. The tragedy of four years previous was fresh in their minds, and fearing a like result caused them to go wild with terror. The chiefs and warriors collected around Tonti beseeching him to protect them from the tomahawks and scalping knives of their enemies in accordance with La Salle's promise. In reply Tonti said his force was not sufficient to afford them protection, but advised them to collect their warriors and defend the town. The French who lived in the town with their families, and a few Indian friends, fled to the fort, while the inhabitants being panic-stricken left in great haste down the river. Soon after their departure the invaders came, but found a barren victory, as not one living soul was left in the town.

When the Iroquois found their intended victims had fled they attacked the fort, and held it in siege six days. For a number of days the Indians continued to fire on the fort from the neighboring cliffs, but without producing any effect. The occupants of the fort not returning the fire emboldened the assailants, and each day they came closer and secreted themselves in the timber near the base of the rock, with the intention, no doubt, of making an assault; but when they came in close range the guns were brought to bear on them, receiving the fire of both musket and cannon. Many were killed, others wounded, while the survivors, being panic-stricken. fled in all haste, leaving their dead and wounded behind. For many days after the Indians were repulsed the French remained within their fortifications, and did not venture down from the rock until convinced that the enemy had left the country.

No Iroquois Indians were ever seen in that vicinity afterward, and they never made another raid on the Illinoisans.

RETURN OF TONTI'S VICTORIOUS ARMY.

In 1687 Tonti, with fifty French soldiers and two hundred Illinois warriors, went to Canada and joined Gen. Denonville in an expedition against the Indians south of Lake Ontario. This army was victorious; many towns along the Mohawk River were burned, and a large number of scalps taken. After completing the victory the army returned to Canada, when Tonti with his soldiers and Indian allies left for Illinois. On their return they were accompanied by a number of emigrant families, among whom were wives, sons and daughters of soldiers and fur traders belonging to the colony. For many weeks the voyageurs in their bark canoes coasted along the lake shores,— at night dragging their frail barks on the beech and sleeping in the open air. On reaching the mouth of Chicago River they ascended it; then crossed the portage into Des Plaines, and down the Illinois River to their destination.

It was a bright, clear morning in midsummer, the silver rays of the sun reflected from the rippling waters of the river as it glided swiftly by. The fresh morning breeze was cooled by passing through branches of forest trees, and the songs of birds added enchantment and loveliness to the surrounding scene. The occupants of Fort St. Louis, after the morning prayer and an exhortation by Father Allouez, were collected along the brink of the rock watching the finny tribe as they sported over the sand and rocks in the clear, shallow water. While thus engaged they were startled by hearing the sound of a bugle up the river, and on looking in that direction they saw the broad stream covered with canoes all filled with human beings. On came this fleet of canoes, with flags flying, drums beating, and the loud cheering of both French and Indians announced the return of Tonti's victorious army. As this large fleet of canoes passed rapidly down the swift current the cannons on the fort boomed forth loud peals of welcome to returning friends.

There was great rejoicing at Fort St. Louis, wives and children of soldiers and fur traders had come thither to join husbands and fathers after many years of separation, and the meeting was an affecting one.

On the following night a ball and wine supper was given in honor of the occasion, and the great hall of the fort rang with martial music, songs, toasts, with various demonstrations of joy. Ladies from fashionable society of Montreal gave an air of refinement to the ball, and such a gay party was never before witnessed in the wilds of the west. Much wine was drank, the sound of music and joyous laughter of the dancers rang forth on the clear night air. Father Allouez, having spent twenty years among savages in the west without mingling in refined society, became so overjoyed by the gay party and effects of the wine that he passed to and fro among the ladies, encircling their waists with his arms and offering to bestow his blessings upon them.

CHAPTER VIII.

LE FORT DES MIAMIS.

IN the year 1684 La Barre, governor of Canada, being jealous of La Salle's power and influence, concocted a plan to defeat his enterprise, and thereby appropriate to himself and friends the great wealth to be derived from the fur trade, under a plea that La Salle had forfeited his charter by granting other parties permits to trade with the Indians. He sent an army officer, Capt. De Bougis, to Illinois with authority to take command of Fort St. Louis. Tonti being in command of the fort at the time, surrendered it to the usurper, who took possession of all the goods and furs at the trading-post also. A few months after Capt. De Bougis assumed command he became convinced that he was holding the fort without authority, consequently he gave it up to Tonti and returned to Canada.

On the following year after De Bougis returned to Canada Capt. Richard Pilette made his appearance at Fort St. Louis. Pilette remained at the fort a number of days without letting his business be known, but when the proper time came he drew from his pocket a commission under the Governor's seal authorizing him to take command. Tonti denied the power of the Governor to appoint a commander, as the fort was private property, having been built and maintained by La Salle at his own expense in accordance with a charter from the King of France. In a pompous manner Pilette proclaimed himself commander of the fort by virtue of his commission, and addressing the soldiers in a tone of authority ordered them to lay hold of Tonti and place him under guard. Tonti with his iron hand knocked down the would-be commander, relieving him of three front teeth, and before the usurper could regain his feet the soldiers carried him outside of the gateway, setting him on the rock and giving him a start downward. The rock being covered with sleet Pilette could not recover his footing or stop his descent, and in that position slid to the bottom, tearing his pantaloons into fragments and bruising himself on the sharp crags of rocks. Capt. Pilette, bruised and bleeding, made his way to La Vautum, where he found sympathy among his countrymen and their Indian friends. With eighteen Frenchmen and fifty warriors he went to Buffalo Rock, and on its summit commenced building a fort in defiance of La Salle's charter or Fort St. Louis.

LE FORT DES MIAMIS.   95

Here he built a block-house, a store-house, and surrounded it with earthworks and palisades. Indians to a large number came here, and built lodges within the stockades, and it became a large town. The place took the name of Le Fort des Miamis, and was occupied by the Indians long after the French left the country. The remains of this fort were plain to be seen in the early settlement of the county, and were mistaken for the relics of Fort St. Louis.*

For many years Pilette traded with the Indians, but was compelled to pay a duty to Fort St. Louis in accordance to La Salle's charter. Having married a squaw he raised a family of half-breed children, to whom he left a large fortune, made in the fur trade. After his death the family removed to Peoria, and one of his grandsons, Louis Pilette, was a claimant for the land where the city now stands. Hypolite Pilette, a great-grandson of the captain, who is now living on the American Bottom, has in his possession many articles that once belonged to his distinguished ancestor. From Hypolite Pilette I obtained

---

* Fifty years ago the relics of this fort were plain to be seen on the summit of Buffalo Rock, and were pointed out by early settlers as the remains of Fort St. Louis. These remains consisted of low earthworks enclosing three sides of about one acre of land, the margin of the rock forming the fourth. The many raids of the Iroquois caused the Indians to take refuge on Buffalo Rock, where they would be secure within the stockades of the fort.

A short distance from the fort were a number of sepulchral mounds, the largest of which, according to tradition, was raised over the grave of Capt. Pilette.

These old relics have been plowed over for many years by Mr. A. Betger, the owner of the land, and most of them leveled down, but still their outlines can be traced out.

most of the traditionary account of Le Fort des Miamis, as well as many other items relating to the French and Indians of former times.

THE LAST OF TONTI.*

For fifteen years after the death of La Salle the fur trade was carried on by Tonti and La Frost. The latter spent most of his time in Canada, and the former at Fort St. Louis, shipping each year a large quantity of furs, and receiving goods in exchange. In 1702 the Governor of Canada, claiming that the traders had forfeited their charter by collecting furs at various points on Lake Michigan, and by force of arms took possession of Fort St. Louis, confiscating to the Government all their stock in trade. By this act of injustice Tonti was not only deprived of his right to command the fort but ruined in fortune. Calling his friends together he took leave of them, saying that he was about to depart from the country never to return. Both French and Indians collected around Tonti beseeching him to remain with them, but he had decided to do otherwise, and with many tokens of friendship he bade them adieu. Accompanied by two companions he boarded a canoe

---

*For the two sketches relating to the death of Tonti and burning of Fort St. Louis I am indebted to Jacques Matte, whose great-grandfather was a soldier in the fort and was present at Tonti's death and burial also when the fort was burned by the Indians a few months afterward.

and started down the river in search of new adventures.

On reaching the lower Mississippi country Tonti joined D'Iberville, and assisted him in establishing a colony. For sixteen years he remained south, part of the time entrusted with an important mission, but when the colony was broken up by sickness and Spanish invasion he became an outcast and a wanderer. Broken down in health, forsaken by friends, and feeling that his end was nigh, he employed two Indians to take him to Fort St. Louis so he could once more look upon the scene of his vigor and manhood, and leave his bones among people by whom he had long been honored and obeyed.

On a warm afternoon in the summer of 1718, while the occupants of Fort St. Louis were lounging around under the shade of evergreens, they discovered a canoe coming up the river rowed by two Indians. In the bottom of the canoe a man lay on a buffalo robe but on nearing the fort he raised himself into a sitting position, and gazed wildly around him. The canoe landed at the base of the rock, and the travelers commenced ascending it. Between the two Indians was a feeble old man whom the conductors held by each arm, and slowly assisted him up the rocky pathway. On reaching the summit the old man was placed on a bunk, where he lay for some time overcome by fatigue and unable to speak. After taking some stimulants he revived, and inquired of those around him who commanded the fort. On being told it was Captain La Mott he gave a sigh saying La Mott was a usurper, and himself the rightful commander. Those in attendance thought him crazy, or his mind wandering, and they bathed his head with cold water. When sufficiently recovered from exhaustion he told them that his name was Tonti, and he had returned here to die.

Sixteen years had made a great change in the appearance of Tonti, and he was scarcely recognized by his most intimate friends. His tall, manly form was bent by disease, his piercing black eyes were dimmed with age, and his raven locks were as white as snow. News of Tonti's arrival spread throughout the country, and French and Indians from distant villages came to see him. But those who knew him while in the vigor of manhood could scarcely be convinced that the feeble old man was the proud, brave and fearless Tonti of former years. A few days after Tonti arrived at the fort he took the sacrament at the hand of a priest, and while looking upon a gold crucifix which was held before his face he breathed his last. A grave was dug on the river bank, at the west end of Starved Rock, in which his remains found a resting-place.

For many years after Tonti's death both French and Indians, while passing up and down the river, would stop to visit the grave, sometimes placing flowers or mementoes on it in memory of him who sleeps beneath.

FORT ST. LOUIS BURNED AND COLONY BROKEN UP.

So long as the fur trade was conducted by Tonti and La Frost the Indians were well pleased, but when it came under the supervision of the Governor of Canada they became dissatisfied. The Governor appointed unscrupulous agents to conduct the trade, who swindled the Indians by selling them worthless articles such as counterfeit jewelry, knives, tomahawks, etc., made of pot metal, but the principal cause of ill feeling was on account of their social relation. A Frenchman having married a young squaw would put her away as soon as he found one more attractive, thus changing his wife at will according to his fancy. Although the priest would not tolerate bigamy among their countrymen, yet they were willing to accept a marriage fee once a month or as often as the applicant desired a new wife. It was the height of a young squaw's ambition to marry a white man, notwithstanding they were liable to be put away at any time. Under the Indian code of morals if a squaw was found unchaste she was punished by cutting off one ear, or branded on the forehead, but there was no law to prevent them from marrying once a week, or as often as an opportunity occurred.

Captain La Mott commanded the fort, and being a man devoid of conscientious scruples converted it into a regular harem, in open violation of both French and Indian code of morals. Young Indian maidens were in the habit of spending nights at the fort under the pretext of being married to the soldiers, returning home in the morning with their heads adorned with worthless trinkets, and their minds poisoned by vile associations. The squaws became so fascinated with the French that many refused to marry among their own people, having come to the conclusion that children were not worth raising unless they had white blood in their veins. Things had come to such a state in their social relation that the head chief, Jero, called a council of chiefs and warriors, at which it was decided to expel the French from among them.

On a bright morning in the latter part of the summer of 1718, while the occupants of Fort St. Louis, after a night of revelry and debauch, were still asleep in their bunks, they were aroused from slumber by the presence of savages. Captain La Mott on awakening from his morning nap was astonished on being confronted by some 300 warriors armed and painted for war. The Captain inquired of Jero, the head chief, the object of their visit, who in reply said they had come to burn the fort. The chief ordered the warriors to fire the buildings, and in a few minutes the block-house, store-house and dwelling were in flames, all of which were consumed. Thus Fort St. Louis was destroyed, after standing thirty-six years, and during that time it was the head center of the French settlement in Illinois. On the destruction of the fort the colony was broken up, some of the settlers returned to Canada, others to Peoria and Cahokia, a few only who were identified with the Indians by marriage and half-breeds continued to live in the town.

Three years after the burning of Fort St. Louis, in 1721, Charlevoix, a Jesuit priest, visited Illinois and found the palisades still standing but no Frenchmen living here.

CHASSAGOAC, AN INDIAN CHIEF.

For forty years Chassagoac, the head chief of the Illinois Indians, was identified with the French colony, and became celebrated as a friend of the white man. He embraced Christianity under the preaching of Marquette, and continued in this faith until the time of his death. On account of his religious faith and fidelity to the French the Bishop of Rouen sent him many presents, consisting of gold images, crosses, crucifixes, with many other emblems of the Christian religion. These presents were kept sacred, many of them worn on his person, and at his death they were buried with him.

In a gallery of the Jesuit collections in the city of Rouen, France, can now be seen a life-size portrait of Chassagoac, which shows him to have been a fine specimen of his race, physically as well as mentally. Whether the artist painted this portrait from life or description is not known, but it is a good representation of the person described in history. This chief died in the year 1714, and a large mound raised over his grave, on which Father Felix erected a cross. Back of the old town of Utica the mound supposed to have been raised over this noted chief can still be seen, as well as the cavity in the earth near by from which the dirt was taken to erect it. About sixty years ago Waba, an Indian chief of some note, learning from tradition that valuable trinkets had been buried in this mound, opened it and robbed it of its treasures.

LOUISIANA COLONY.

This colony, as has been previously stated, was founded by La Salle at Fort St. Louis in the year 1682 under a charter from Louis XIV, and called

Louisiana in honor to his name. The colony remained here until 1718, a period of thirty-six years, and had it continued permanently La Salle county would have been the oldest settled place in the Mississippi Valley.

In 1711 the King of France gave Crozat a patent covering all of the Louisiana country, over which he was to have control for twenty years. Col. La Mott, an agent of Crozat, took possession of the country, assuming the title of governor, and made Kaskaskia the capital. A large corps of miners came from France, and two years were spent in the northern country in searching for gold and silver, but without success. Copper and lead were found in great abundance, but none of the precious metal for which they were in search. After five years' experience in mining and trading with the Indians Crozat found it unprofitable, consequently he surrendered his patent to the crown, and Col. La Mott with many of the miners returned to France.

In 1717 a new patent was granted to a Louisiana company, with George Law, a Scotch banker of Paris, at its head; and by this company Fort Chartres was built. This company issued large grants of land to each village, including many thousand acres known as common field and commons. They also made and enforced just laws regulating village ordinances, which superseded some of the arbitrary code brought about by the Jesuit priests.

FRENCH SETTLEMENT AROUND FORT ST. LOUIS.

According to tradition, a number of cabins were built around the base of Starved Rock and occupied by people engaged in the fur trade. In my researches among the descendants of the early pioneers I found three families whose ancestors lived at Fort St. Louis, and from whom I obtained many of the items given in this sketch. When the fort was burned in 1718 all the settlers left for other places; the cabins rotted down, but the underground furnaces for heating them still remain, nine of which have been discovered within the last few years.

By an order of Father Zenobe, all persons belonging to the colony, both soldiers and civilians, were required to assemble once a day in the chapel of the fort for prayers, and for that purpose men, women and children each morning were seen ascending the Rock.

The cemetery was located on the river bank at the west end of the Rock; and here on this romantic spot, shaded by outspreading oaks, overlooking the broad, rapid stream, Henri de Tonti, two Jesuit priests, with a number of soldiers and civilians, found a long resting-place. In the early settlement of the country human bones were seen sticking out of the river bank at this place, where the dirt had been washed away by a flood.

The French settlers cultivated an island in the river and a field on the prairie north of it, also a small piece of ground west of the Rock, between the river and bluff, showed unmistakable marks of having been cultivated. A large portion of the grain and vegetables to supply the garrison were raised by the French and half-breeds on the Indian fields at La Vantum, while the meat, which consisted of buffalo, elk and deer, was furnished by Indian hunters.

On the north side of the river, a short distance above Starved Rock, are three sulphur springs, one of which is large, boiling up among white sand and sending forth an immense volume of water. Indians from a distance came here to be healed of their maladies, and during the summer the springs were surrounded with camping-tents. These poor benighted people entertained the same foolish notions as people of the present day regarding the medical qualities of mineral water

In 1853 a large stone building, called "Sulphur

Spring Hotel," was built here, with the expectation of making it a great watering-place. Notwithstanding a large amount of money was spent in building and advertising by those interested, they did not succeed in making it a Saratoga or a Homburg.

CHAPTER IX.

JESUIT MISSIONARIES OF THE WEST.

THE Jesuit missionaries in their zeal abandoned home, friends and all the comforts of civilization for the purpose of converting heathens. Governed by religious fanaticism they carried their faith and works to the most remote parts of the west, and among the lowest degraded savages. They were found along the ice-bound shores of Lake Superior, clothed in deer or buffalo skins, and with snow-shoes, struggling through thick timber, or crossing wide prairies, to lodge in a filthy, smoky den with savages. Again at the south among bogs and swamps filled with vermin and wild beasts they administered the sacrament to painted and plumed proselytes. To accomplish their purposes they traveled through various parts of the country from Canada to the Gulf of Mexico,— sometimes suffering from cold and hunger, deprived of all the luxuries of civilized life, all for the purpose of converting the heathen and saving their souls from eternal perdition. These enthusiastic priests with their black robes could be seen toiling with half naked natives building lodges, or forcing their canoe up the rapid stream; sometimes carrying their baggage on their backs to and from distant villages, or lounging around a camp-fire on a bear or buffalo skin amid scores of squalling papooses and half famished dogs. The stories of their labors are replete with romance, miracles of heroic self-sacrifices, and with daring adventures.

Everywhere these priests were the pioneers of the French settlements in the west, keeping in advance of civilization, and preparing the way for a friendly intercourse between the white and red man. Many of these missionaries were well educated, with superior mental ability, possessed of wealth, which made them efficient bearers of the cross, and whose whole life was spent in converting heathens.

Father Marest in his correspondence says, "Our life is spent in rambling through thick timber, among briers and thorns, crossing wide prairies, climbing over hills, or paddling a canoe across lakes or up rapid rivers, to save the poor benighted Indian from eternal perdition."

Father Nicollet lived twenty years among savages, most of the time without meeting a white man, and became an Indian in dress, habit and language. Still he remained a zealous Catholic, and at last returned to civilization because he could not live without the sacrament.

From the Jesuit missionaries the Indians learned the story of Christ's crucifixion, and with a trembling voice repeated it to their friends. They not only received baptism from the hands of the priest but allowed themselves to be sprinkled with holy water, which they were taught to believe blotted out all past sins, and saved them from everlasting punishment. The medals, crosses and crucifixes which the priest gave the warriors pleased their fancy, as they were fond of adorning their persons with glittering trinkets, and with these representations of man's salvation suspended from their necks they remain heathens still. In addition to decorating their persons with emblems of Christianity some of the warriors wore a necklace made of dried skeleton fingers taken from an enemy whom they had slain in battle. The former trinkets represented their religion, and the latter their patriotism.

Father Meurain, the last of the Jesuit priests in Illinois, died at Prairie du Rocher in 1778, and the monument over his grave can still be seen. In France and her territories the order of Jesuits was suppressed in 1764, when most of the priests in Illinois returned to their native country. But by the solicitation of the Indians, with whom he had labored for a long time, Father Meurain consented to remain, and among them he ended his days. Father Meurain was a man of fine literary attainments, and wrote a manuscript dictionary of the French and Indian languages, which is preserved in the antiquarian collection at Rouen.

FATHER SENAT AND COMRADE BURNED AT THE STAKE.

One of the most devoted Jesuit priests in Illinois was Father Senat, who spent a long life among savages for the purpose of converting them to Christianity, and at last fell a victim of these ruthless barbarians. This zealous priest lived many years at Peoria, where he built a chapel and dedicated it to the Holy Virgin. He preached at different villages along the river, where he had many converts, and exercised great influence over his red brethren. While on a visit to a neighboring village a war party returned from the battle-field with a number of prisoners, and made preparation to burn them at the stake in accordance to Indian custom. Father Senat, on finding all efforts to save the prisoners from the flames a failure, offered himself a sacrifice to die in their stead a ransom for the captives. This proposition had the desired effect. The prisoners were liberated, furnished with many presents, and returned to their people.

FATHER SENAT AND COMRADE BURNED. 111

In the spring of 1736 D'Artaguette, Governor of Illinois, collected all the French troops in the territory, with about one thousand Indian allies, and with them went to Louisiana to assist Governor Bainville in prosecuting a war against the Chickasaw Indians. Among these recruits was Capt. Vincennes with a small company of soldiers from St. Vincent on the Wabash, which place now bears the name of the valiant captain. Among the Indian allies from the Illinois River were many of Father Senat's converts, and he was prevailed upon to accompany them in their excursion to the south.

This expedition descended the Mississippi River to the lower Chickasaw bluffs, from which they crossed the country to Tallahatchie River, where they expected to meet the army under Bainville from Louisiana. But these troops failed to come to time agreeable to appointment, and d'Artaguette, not being able to restrain his Indian allies any longer, was forced to attack the enemy. The army was defeated, the Indian allies fled, while the French were taken prisoners and burned at the stake. While the flames encircled their bodies Father Senat passed from one to the other amid blazing fagots, exhorting his friends to die as became Frenchmen and Christians, and while they were racking with torture he administered to his dying countrymen the last rites of the Catholic church. The Indians offered to liberate Father Senat, but he disdained their clemency, telling them his work in this world was done, and he desired to be sacrificed for his Master's sake.

EARLY FRENCH SETTLEMENTS IN ILLINOIS.

The first permanent settlers in Illinois came from Canada, and they were connected either with the Jesuit mission or fur trade. In after years emigrants came direct from France by the way of New Orleans, and established colonies in different Indian villages on the American Bottom. All the settlers lived in villages, and their farms were in a common field, in accordance with the custom of their native country. The leaders of the French colonies were men of education and energy of character, while the masses were illiterate and ignorant, having no enterprise and but little property; nevertheless they were frank, open-hearted, happy people. They took possession of so much of the vacant land around them as they could till, but no more, and appeared to have had no desire to accumulate wealth. Their agricultural implements were rude, mostly of their own manufacture, and the same kind of tools are now in use by some of their descendants. The early settlers lived in harmony with the Indians, intermarrying among them, and in part adopting their habits and customs. For forty years they built no forts, and those erected in after years were not intended for protection against Indian hostilities but from the fear of Spanish invasion, France and Spain being then at war.

The oldest document found in Kaskaskia (except the church records) is dated June 18, 1725, and contains the signatures of fifty persons, who are represented as heads of families. This old document is in the form of a petition to the King of France for assistance,— setting forth the suffering condition of the people on account of the great flood the year before, which washed away most of the improvements, and obliged the people to flee to the bluffs.

By the Louisiana Company horses were brought from the Spanish settlements in Mexico to take the place of Indian ponies, and cattle, hogs, sheep, and chickens were brought from Canada. Wild geese, ducks and turkeys were domesticated, and from this stock most of the fowls of the present day sprang. It is said two pigs were brought from Montreal to Cahokia in a canoe, and from these pigs hogs to supply the different settlements originated. Many efforts were made to domesticate buffalo, but it proved a failure, as the tame ones would go off with wild herds. But they succeeded in crossing them with cattle, and at the present time some of the progeny show strong marks of buffalo origin, and their pelts are tanned for robes. Horses ran in large droves in the canebreaks along the Mississippi River, became wild, and in after years many of them were caught with a lasso and brought into use.

In 1721 Phillip Raynault brought five hundred slaves from St. Domingo to Fort Chartres, and by this means slavery was introduced into Illinois. Raynault with a large number of slaves and a few of his countrymen ascended the Mississippi River to the lead mines, and erected a furnace for smelting lead on or near the present site of Galena. A portion of this lead was shipped to New Orleans, and sold to the Spaniards in Mexico.

Father Vevier, a Jesuit missionary, writing from Prairie du Rocher under date of June 10, 1750, says "there are between the Mississippi and Kaskaskia Rivers, within twenty-one leagues, five French and three Indian villages. Most of the French settlers till the soil, raising wheat, maize, with various other products, some of which are shipped to New Orleans, where it finds a ready market."

In the early settlement of the country the French made wine from the wild grape, but in after years they cultivated vineyards, and built wine-presses. The buffalo was of great service to the early pioneers; the flesh they used for food, the hides for robes or tanned into leather, and the hair they spun and wove into a fine fabric for clothing.

The Royal Louisiana Company gave large tracts of land to each village which belonged jointly to the inhabitants, and this title has been confirmed by subsequent laws. These grants were divided into two tracts, known as Common Field and Commons, and included many thousand acres to each village. The common field consisted in farm land all fenced into one field, the boundaries of each person's premises were designated by landmarks, and these tracts belonged to the occupant in fee simple, and could be bought and sold the same as other landed property. A village ordinance was in force regarding making and repairing fences, the time of excluding stock in the spring, gathering the crops, and opening the field for pasture in the fall. The commons was a tract of land granted to each town for wood and pasture, of which every owner of a village lot has an interest. The French villages at the time of early settlement were governed by the priest, who, besides attending to their spiritual wants, dispensed justice, and from his decision there was no appeal. Although the authority of the priest was absolute there appears to have been no abuse of this power, as the holy father watched over his flock with paternal care.

EARLY SETTLEMENT OF ST. LOUIS.

In 1763 Pierre Laclade obtained from the governor of Louisiana a charter giving him the exclusive right to trade with the Indians on the west side of the upper Mississippi River. Laclade organized a company at New Orleans under the title of Laclade, Maxon & Co., and aboard of boats loaded with goods for the Indian market ascended the river in search of a suitable place to locate. On reaching Fort Chartres the goods were stored, and Laclade with some of his party, accompanied by two young men named Pierre and Aguste Chouteau, ascended the river in a canoe in search of a good site for a town, and on the 15th of February, 1764, their tents were pitched at St. Louis, which was the commencement of the great city in the west. Here a cluster of cabins was built, enclosed by stockades, and occupied by traders and hunters. Many of the inhabitants of Illinois towns crossed the river and located at St. Louis in order to be under the rule of their native country.

When Captain Stirling, in accordance with a treaty, took possession of Fort Chartres in July, 1765, its former commander, Captain St. Ange, with the French troops and military stores, removed to St. Louis, and for a number of years the colony was under French rule, notwithstanding the country had been ceded to Spain some time before.

In 1780 St. Louis was attacked by a large body of Indians, accompanied by a few British soldiers from Detroit, but they were repulsed by the citizens and soldiers.

BRITISH RULE IN ILLINOIS.

In the summer of 1764 Major Loftus with three hundred British soldiers ascended the Mississippi River in boats from Bayou Manchea to take possession of Illinois, as France had ceded it to England a short time before. While these troops were on their way up the river, and before reaching their destination, they were attacked and defeated by a body of Indians, which compelled them to abandon the enterprise and return to the fort at Bayou Manchea.

In the spring of 1765 an expedition under Captain Croghan left Fort Pitt to take possession of Illinois, but on reaching the mouth of the Wabash they were taken prisoners by the Shawnee Indians, and carried to a village near Vincennes. In the following fall the third expedition against Illinois left Fort Pitt, under the command of Captain Stirling, who took possession of the country without opposition, and from that time the British flag waved over Fort Chartres. In the following year Captain Stirling died, and different ones at short intervals acted as governors of Illinois, the last one, **M.** Rocheblauc, was in command when Colonel Clark took possession of the country. The British rule was very unpopular with the French, many of them went west of the Mississippi so they could be under the laws of their native country. This change of government displeased the Indians, and they would have attacked the British for the purpose of driving them out of the country if their friends among the French had not counseled otherwise. When the British took possession of Illinois Captain Pitman, of the army, by the authority of his government visited all the French villages except Peoria, and gave a description of them, including population, trade, public buildings, etc. The French inhabitants were living in six villages, all except one on the American Bottom, and estimates the inhabitants at three thousand, the most of whom were engaged in agricultural pursuits.

CHAPTER X.

TOM BRADY'S WILD ADVENTURES.

THOMAS R. BRADY, better known as Tom Brady, was a native of Pennsylvania, and a brother of Captain Samuel Brady, who distinguished himself as an Indian fighter in the border wars of Ohio. Brady was a reckless fellow, fond of wild adventures, a great hunter (spending much of his time in the woods in search of bear and panthers), and occasionally exchanging a shot with an Indian. In the summer of 1776 Tom Brady went to Cahokia accompanied by three other young men as wild and reckless as himself, and who were willing to accompany him in any enterprise he might undertake. On the following summer Brady fitted out an expedition, consisting of sixteen soldiers including himself, for the purpose of capturing the British garrison at St. Joseph. This little band of adventurers he called the western division of the Continental army, and with it he intended to attack and capture the British garrison. Among those who took a part in this remarkable expedition was M. Boismenue, a native of Cahokia, and to whose grandson I am indebted for many incidents given in this narrative. Many of Brady's recruits were French half-breed members of the Catholic church, and they were unwilling to embark in so hazardous an enterprise unless accompanied by a priest to absolve them from their sins. Father Beson, an old, bald-headed priest, was prevailed on to accompany the troops, and before leaving Cahokia he offered up prayers to the throne of grace for their success.

Brady's little band, armed and equipped for war, — on board of three canoes — left for St. Joseph, about four hundred miles distant. On reaching an elevated piece of ground, on the west side of the Illinois River, below the mouth of Bureau Creek, where tradition says a century before Father Hennepin landed from his boat, raised a cross, and consecrated the place to the Virgin Mary. Father Beson could not be prevailed upon to pass this hallowed spot without offering up prayers and saying mass. Here the adventurers landed from their canoes, and a day was spent in preaching, praying, taking the sacrament, and singing songs of praise. causing the wild woods to resound with their melody. On reaching the mouth of Chicago River the party spent another day in religious exercises around a large wooden cross, said to occupy the spot where Father

Marquette erected one more than a century before. After many weeks of toil and exposure in forcing their frail crafts up the Illinois and Des Plaines Rivers, and buffeting the angry winds and waves on Lake Michigan, they reached their destination. The fort at St. Joseph was garrisoned by twenty-one soldiers, while the attacking party consisted of only sixteen; but Brady, relying on the prestige of surprise, felt confident of success. Accordingly they attacked the fort during the night while all were asleep, and the astonished soldiers, without making any resistance, surrendered themselves prisoners of war.

A few days after taking possession of the fort at St. Joseph the victors learned that two companies of British soldiers with many Indian allies were marching upon it. On receiving this intelligence Brady and his comrades in all haste loaded their canoes with furs and merchandise (taken out of the fort) and left for home; but on reaching the mouth of Calumet River they were overtaken by three hundred British and Indians. Here a battle was fought, at which Brady's army was defeated, having two killed and two wounded; one made his escape, while the remainder were made prisoners and carried back to St. Joseph. Some time after, becoming a prisoner, Tom Brady made his escape, and on foot, and alone, he traveled through the forest back to his former home in Pennsylvania.

After reaching his old home in Pennsylvania Tom Brady raised a company of scouts, and with them made many excursions into the Indian country, in one of which he was severely wounded. He joined Colonel Crawford's expedition against the Indians on the Sandusky River, and participated in that disastrous affair. On arriving in the enemy's country Colonel Crawford sent Brady, accompanied by two companions as daring as himself, forward to reconnoiter while the army remained in camp awaiting their return. When the scouts came near the Indian village on the bank of the Sandusky River they heard loud whoops and yells, and occasionally firing of guns. With great caution the scouts crawled on their hands and knees through the thick underbrush until they came in plain view of a large body of warriors engaged in a scalp-dance. By the side of these dancers were seen three white men on horseback looking on and enjoying the sport. These men were recognized by the scouts as Alexander McKee, Simon and James Girty, three noted desperadoes.

At one time the Girtys lived in the same neighborhood with Brady, and consequently he was well acquainted with them. As Tom Brady looked at

Simon Girty he was reminded of the many raids in which that cut-throat had led the Indians into his own neighborhood, murdering defenseless women and children. In one of these raids Brady's father and one of his brothers were killed, and bringing a rifle to his shoulder was about to shoot him from his horse. But before Brady could effect his bloody designs one of his comrades caught the gun and thereby prevented the rash act, as it would have been certain death to all of the party. After the war closed Tom Brady returned to Illinois, again became a resident of Cahokia, and in the year 1790 was sheriff of St. Clair county.

On a recent visit to Cahokia I spent some time among the tombs in the old church-yard where so many distinguished early pioneers were buried. Among the graves distinguished by sandstone slabs was one to the memory of Thomas R. Brady.

TWO EXPEDITIONS AGAINST ST. JOSEPH, AND ONE AGAINST DETROIT.

In the spring of 1778, two months before the country was invaded by Virginians under the command of Colonel Clark, a Frenchman named Puelette Maize, of Kaskaskia, enlisted about three hundred men in different French towns, and marched through the country to St. Joseph, which they took by surprise. All the fur, pelts and merchandise found at the fort and trading-houses were carried off as trophies of war, and divided among the soldiers. After collecting all the valuables to be found at the post the victors with their spoil returned home, and were disbanded. It is generally believed that this expedition was fitted out more for plunder than patriotism, as Congress in after years refused to recompense those engaged in it.

In the fall of 1780 La Balme, a native of France, raised a small company of soldiers at Kaskaskia for the purpose of taking Detroit. At Vincennes they were reinforced by a few of their countrymen, and from here they marched direct for the British post. While encamped on the Maumee River they were attacked by a large body of Miami Indians, led by a British officer, when La Balme and many of his soldiers were killed, and the rest taken prisoners.

In June, 1781, Don Eugenie Pierre, a Spaniard of St. Louis, with sixty-five soldiers, most of whom were French who lived at Cahokia, marched against St. Joseph, as England and Spain were then at war. The fort was taken without resistance, when the commanding officers went through with the ceremony of taking possession of all the lake country in the name of the King of Spain. A few days after performing this idle ceremony the Spanish commander' learned that British troops were on their way from Detroit to reinforce St. Joseph, consequently the troops left the conquered territory in all haste, and returned to St. Louis.

PAT. KENNEDY AND COMRADES IN SEARCH OF COPPER MINES.

For many years the citizens of Kaskaskia and other French towns believed there were copper mines somewhere in the upper Illinois country, as specimens of pure metal, in a native state, were frequently brought there for sale by the Indians. On July 23, 1773, Kennedy, with a party of adventurers, left Kaskaskia in a boat and ascended the Illinois River in search of copper mines. On the 7th of August they reached Peoria, where they found the stockades of the fort burned, but the block-houses still standing. On arriving at the foot of the rapids, and finding the current too strong to ascend, they left their boat and proceeded up the river on foot forty-five miles further. Before reaching the mouth of the Fox River they noticed a number of high, rocky cliffs, one of which (Starved Rock) has figured extensively in the history and traditions of the country. On an island thirty miles above the mouth of Fox River they fell in with a party of French traders, who brought them down the river in their canoes to the place where their boat had been left. While at the foot of the rapids they fell in with a Frenchman by the name of Jennette, who piloted them in an excursion through the country in search of copper mines, but finding none these adventurers went aboard of their boat and returned to Kaskaskia, after being absent about four months.

Kennedy published a journal of his travels up the river, which contains many things of interest and confirms some of the traditions given elsewhere. This journal gives a geographical and topographical description of the country, size and names of rivers, lakes, bluffs, rapids, etc. It speaks of a saline spring by a lake, where the French and Indians were engaged in making salt; also refers to a cliff of rocks near the mouth of Fox River, from which the French obtained their mill stones. On the large meadows were seen herds of buffalo, elk and deer, while pelicans, swans, geese and ducks were swimming in the rivers and lakes. The journal refers to Peoria Lake, town and fort, but throws no light on the history of the French settlement at this place, says nothing about the size of the town, nor its general appearance at that time.

CHAPTER XI.

COLONEL CLARK'S CONQUEST OF ILLINOIS.

ON the 4th of July, 1778, during the shades of the night, the citizens of Kaskaskia were astonished by hearing it proclaimed throughout the town "If any man enter the streets he shall be shot." Next morning soldiers were seen along the streets of the town, and the stars and stripes instead of the lion and unicorn waived from the flag-staff on Fort Gage. The people were in a transport of joy, bells rang, patriotic songs were sung, while demonstrations of rejoicing with tokens of mirth and gayety reigned throughout the town. The annals of romance furnish nothing more remarkable than the achievement of this bloodless conquest of Illinois. The origin of this expedition, the long, tedious journey performed by the adventurers, with its perils and hardships, the manner of attack on the British garrison, and its final success, appears more like a story of fiction than of reality.

Kaskaskia at the time of the revolutionary war contained about 250 houses, being the largest and most important town west of the Alleghany mountains, and not only the seat of government of Illinois but the center of trade, wealth and political influence.

Although an account of Colonel Clark's conquest of Illinois has been written many times, and appears in almost every western history, nevertheless a very important matter has been overlooked, and the real facts relating thereto have never been published. The early historian, probably ignorant of the facts, fell into an error, and subsequent ones copied after him. People are now living in Randolph county whose ancestors were a party to the secret movements of the patriots of Illinois, and whose traditions to some extent supply the missing links in history, as well as correct its errors. The people in Illinois being far away from the seat of war knew very little of what had transpired at the east, but they hated the British yoke, embraced the first opportunity to throw it off, and their manner of doing it will be shown in the sequel.

In the summer of 1777 John Duff, a resident of Martinsburg, Virginia, in his rambles in the west came to Kaskaskia and remained here for some months engaged in hunting along the river. Duff being of French descent spoke that language, mingled freely with the people, and found them very much dissatisfied with the British rule, and only waited for an opportunity to change the government. Late in the fall Duff returned home, and while on his way, at the falls of Ohio, he fell in with George Roger Clark, a Kentucky pioneer, and told him of the state of affairs in Illinois. Clark became fired with enthusiasm. Seeing an opportunity, as he thought, of immortalizing himself, he accompanied Duff to Williamsburg, and together they laid the case before Patrick Henry, then Governor of Virginia. The governor and his counselors after hearing Duff's statements agreed to send an armed force to that distant country to take possession of the British post. Clark received a commission of lieutenant-colonel, appointed commander in chief of this expedition, and authorized to enlist 500 men for that purpose. Colonel Clark commenced enlisting his men for, as he represented it, the defense of Kentucky, keeping the true destination a secret. The governor issued orders to the commander of Fort Pitt for arms, military stores, and boats for transportation.

In the spring of 1778 three companies of volunteers were collected at Fort Pitt, and in four boats they descended the river to the Falls of Ohio, where they expected to be joined by a company of Kentuckians. Being detained here some time waiting for. recruits a part of one company deserted, and it was the middle of June before they were ready to proceed on their journey. Clark's army consisted of four companies in all, one hundred and fifty-three men, and when their true destination was announced it created much enthusiasm among the volunteers. After dispatching a messenger to Williamsburg notifying Governor Henry of their departure the troops went aboard of their boats and proceeded down the river.

John Duff returned to Illinois early in the spring to prepare the way for Clark's reception, and also to make arrangements to meet the army with a competent guide at the mouth of Tennessee River. On Duff's arrival at Kaskaskia a consultation was held with a few leading patriots, M. Gibault, the priest, among the number, when it was agreed to keep everything a secret, leaving the masses in ignorance of what they expected to transpire. Duff, with John Saunders, a noted hunter, and two Frenchmen, provided with tents, arms, provisions, etc., left Kaskaskia in a canoe, leaving the impression among the people that they were going to hunt bear and elk along the Ohio River. The hunters descended the Mississippi, and forced their frail barque up the swift current of the Ohio to the mouth of the Tennessee River, where they awaited the arrival of the army.

Here on the bank of the river they erected a bark shanty, occupying their time hunting during the daytime, and keeping up a bonfire at night so the boats might not pass without knowing of their presence. Days passed away without hearing anything from the army, and the hunters had about come to the conclusion that the project had failed when four boats filled with soldiers, and flags flying, came around a bend in the river. The hunters fired a salute, which was returned by the soldiers, who with martial music, loud cheering, rounded to their boats and came on shore. After passing down the river a few miles farther, near the ruins of old Fort Massac, they secreted their boats in the mouth of a creek, and taking all their baggage on their backs they proceeded across the country to Kaskaskia, one hundred and twenty miles distant.

John Saunders acted as guide for Clark's army, but in passing through the country among the lakes and swamps of Cache River he lost his reckoning, and days were spent in rambling through thick timber, among bogs and briers, without knowing where they were.

Some of the soldiers believed the pilot a traitor, and threatened to put him to death, but he asserted his innocence, and asked for an escort to accompany him in searching out the way. After rambling about all day through groves and prairies Saunders at last exclaimed " I know that point of timber, and beyond it is Kaskaskia."

Fort Gage, at Kaskaskia, was garrisoned at that time by twenty soldiers under the command of Governor Rocheblave, but no sentinels were kept on duty; being, as they believed, far away from the enemy, it was thought unnecessary.

Colonel Clark on coming within a few miles of Kaskaskia, in the afternoon, remained secreted in the thick timber until late at night, when he divided his army into three parts, two of which took possession of the town, while the third, commanded by himself, marched on the fort. A soldier who was in sympathy with the Americans, and entrusted with the secret, conducted the troops through a back gate into the fort, where they found a light burning but all the inmates asleep. The commander had no knowledge of what was going on until awakened by Captain Kenton informing him that he was a prisoner. The soldiers rejoiced at this turn of affairs, all of whom took the oath of allegiance to the United States Government, and a number of them joined Clark's army. Governor Rocheblave was probably the only royal person in Illinois. Being in a bad humor he cursed the Yankees, the treacherous French, and his disloyal soldiers. The refractory governor was put in irons, and under the charge of Captain Montgomery carried to Williamsburg, the capital of Virginia, where he was kept a prisoner of war until exchanged. His slaves were sold by Colonel Clark, and the proceeds being considered prize money was divided among the soldiers. The wife of Governor Rocheblave, on the night the fort was taken, destroyed all the public papers, including the archives of the territory, which gave people much trouble in after years. She remained at Kaskaskia for some time after her husband was made a prisoner, and Governor Henry wrote to Colonel Todd to see that she was provided for.

Colonel Clark dispatched a company of men under the command of Captain Bowman, accompanied by many citizens of Kaskaskia, to Prairie du Rocher, Cahokia, and other villages, and everywhere the invaders were received with acclamations of joy.

Ten days after Clark's army arrived at Kaskaskia M. Gibault, the village priest and leader of the patriots in Illinois, accompanied by a few friends, went to Vincennes, and explained to his French countrymen the state of affairs in Illinois. All the people of the village assembled at their church, headed by their priest, and agreed to throw off the British rule, taking the oath of allegiance to the United States Government and the commonwealth of Virginia.

There was no garrison at the fort, the troops having been removed a short time before, consequently a commander was appointed from among the church communicants, the British flag taken down, and the stars and stripes put in its place.

On the first of August M. Gibault and party returned to Kaskaskia, after an absence of fourteen days, with the joyful intelligence of having adjusted everything at Vincennes in favor of American interests, which caused much rejoicing among the people. Colonel Clark sent Captain Helm to Vincennes to take charge of the fort, but a short time afterward the British troops, commanded by Colonel Hamilton, took possession of the place and made Captain Helm and a private named Henry prisoners of war.

In February following Colonel Clark, with the combined forces of Virginians, French and Indians, retook the place, and again the stars and stripes waived from the flag-staff of the fort, all of which is a matter of history.

France at that time was an ally of the United States, the first nation to acknowledge her independence, and all the inhabitants of Illinois were in union with the mother country. The patriots of Illinois had already fitted out two expeditions, one commanded by Tom Brady and the other by Puelett Maize, both of which captured the British post at St. Joseph. The people everywhere through the French settlements hailed Colonel Clark as a liberator, and furnished his army with provision free of charge as he had no money to pay for supplies. Many of the French joined his army; a company was raised at Kaskaskia commanded by Captain Charlesville, and another at Cahokia under Captain McCarty, and both of these companies rendered good service on the Wabash in retaking the British post at Vincennes.

While Colonel Clark was engaged in reorganizing his army for the purpose of marching against Vincennes an unexpected trouble arose which for a time threatened to defeat his enterprise. The Indians had always been opposed to the British rule in Illinois, and would have made war against them had not the council of their French friends prevailed. When Clark's army came into the country the Indians were told that the Americans were the friends and allies of the French, and they would live together as one people. For awhile this appears to have given satisfaction, but the stars and stripes continued to float from the flag-staff of the forts at Kaskaskia, and Cahokia, and the Indians insisted that these should be taken down and French flags put in their place. In order to reconcile the Indians a council was called at Cahokia for the purpose of effecting a compromise, but the leading chiefs insisted that the French should be reinstated in authority. For a time the Indians refused to accept of any compromise that did not put the French in authority, and an attempt was made among the leaders to assassinate Colonel Clark. Previous to the meeting of this council Colonel Clark had sent Captain Helm to the great chief Grand Door, for the purpose of effecting a compromise, and he agreed on conditions that if his band were furnished a certain amount of goods at a given time the Americans would not be molested. A messenger arrived at the council with the intelligence of Grand Door having consented to let the Americans keep possession of the country, the chiefs of other bands acquiesced, and a reconciliation was effected.

As soon as the Indian trouble was settled Colonel Clark collected his forces, marched to the Wabash, and took possession of Vincennes.

Colonel Clark has been much eulogized for bravery and heroism in the conquest of Illinois, but the fact is, no enemy opposed him, therefore he took possession of a country occupied by friends, as has already been shown.

CHAPTER XII.

PONTIAC.

PROBABLY no North American Indian has acquired such fame and notoriety, and whose power was so much felt by the early settlers of the country, as Pontiac. This Indian, so often referred to by historians, was born and raised near Detroit, and for many years head chief of the Ottawa Indians. Like Phillip of Mount Hope his power and influence extended over neighboring tribes, which made him more like a king than a chief. So long as the French controlled the fur trade of the lake country Pontiac lived on friendly terms with his white neighbors, but when the English took possession of the country he denounced them as enemies. While Major Rogers, of the British army, was marching westward with a regiment of soldiers to take possession of Detroit he was met by Pontiac, who inquired of the commander by what authority he invaded the country. With his tall figure raised to its full height, and holding his right hand before the face of Major Rogers, said to him "I stand in your path, and you can go no farther without my permission."

However, Pontiac allowed the English to take possession of the French trading-posts along the lakes, and for a time appeared friendly, but a few years afterward he made war on the invaders with the intention of driving them from the country. He united with him many of the neighboring tribes, forming with them an alliance, which is known in history as "Pontiac's Conspiracy," and a long, bloody war resulted from it. In order to carry on the war successfully he issued checks cut out of birch bark, on which were painted a picture of an otter, and calling for various amounts payable in furs or pelts. These checks were taken by different tribes in payment for munitions of war, and all of them redeemed according to promise.

Pontiac, according to accounts, was an Indian of gigantic stature, with a towering intellect, and exercised almost unlimited power over his people. He pretended to commune with the Great Spirit, who on one occasion said to him "Why do you let these dogs in red clothing take possession of your country; rise in your might and drive them from the land." At another time, in addressing his warriors, said: "Although the red-coats have conquered the French they have not conquered us; we are not slaves nor squaws, and as long as the Great Spirit is our ruler we will maintain our rights. These lakes and these forests were given us by our fathers, and we will part with them only with our lives."

For a time Pontiac was victorious, but eventually the fortune of war turned against him, many of the allies abandoned the cause, which compelled him to make overtures for peace. In 1766 he attended the great Indian council at Oswego, brought about by Sir William Johnson, and here signed a treaty of peace, in which he agreed to bury the tomahawk forever. On returning from this council to his native forest in Michigan Pontiac prevailed on many of his friends to accompany him westward, telling them he could not think of living neighbors to these red-coated dogs,— meaning the British. About two hundred warriors with their families consented to emigrate, and with this little band of followers the great chief left forever his native land. With this remnant of his tribe Pontiac came to Illinois, and located a village on the Kankakee River. This band formed an alliance with the Pottawatomies, who occupied at that time the lake and Wabash countries, and from that time they became as one people.

AN ERROR OF HISTORY.

The great mistake made by early historians in relation to the fate of Pontiac has been copied by every writer of western annals, but when all the facts are examined this error must be admitted by every candid reader. I have given this matter much attention by collecting the traditions both among the French and Indians relating to it, and these accounts are susceptible of only one conclusion.

In the fall of 1769 a large, prepossessing Ottawa Indian, dressed in a French uniform, with a big white feather in his cap, came to St. Louis, and represented himself to the commander of the fort, Captain St. Ange, as Pontiac. For a number of days this Indian remained at the fort, drinking whisky, boasting of his great exploits, and telling of the many scalps taken by his own hands. Pierre Chouteau, a young Indian trader of St. Louis, became very much interested in this pompous chief, made him many presents, and in return for these articles the chief promised that in future his people should trade only with Chouteau's agents.

This Indian after remaining some days at St. Louis took a canoe and went to Cahokia, where he was much lionized by French Indians and half-breeds, all of whom believed him to be the great Ottawa chief, Pontiac. Indians from a neighboring village came to see him and listen to his boasting harangues, in which he stated his plans of uniting all the tribes of the west in a war, drive the British from the country, and restore to the French all their former trading-posts. An English trader at Cahokia, named Williamson, being afraid that the reputed Pontiac would persuade his new-made friends to destroy his stock-in-trade, gave a drunken Indian a barrel of whisky to assassinate him, and while the pompous Indian was sitting on the ground at the root of a tree in drunken revelry, explaining to those around him the plans by which he intended to drive the red-coats from the country, this assassin employed by Williamson came up behind him and buried his tomahawk in his skull. After the assassination Captain St. Ange caused the remains to be brought to St. Louis and buried near the fort. Pierre Chouteau, out of respect for the fallen chief, caused a mound to be raised over the grave in accordance with Indian custom, on which was placed a stone with the inscription of the name, time of his death, etc.

Many years after the event above related Pierre and his brother, Auguste Chouteau, having extended their trade into the upper Illinois River country, learned from the Indians the true fate of Pontiac, and on being convinced that the Indian buried at the fort was an impostor removed the stone placed to his memory and leveled down the mound.

An account of the killing of Pontiac at Cahokia found its way into newspapers of that day, and the chief coming to his death about the same time accounts for this error in history.

Both history and tradition agree that the war against the Illinois Indians grew out of the assassination of Pontiac, but the former fails to show any connection between the two events. History says Pontiac was killed by a Kaskaskia Indian in a drunken row at Cahokia, and in avenging this crime a war was inaugurated against the Illinois Indians. The Kaskaskia Indians were not engaged in the war with the allied forces which terminated so fatally to the northern bands, and they continued to live in the country for more than fifty years after that occurrence. The Kaskaskia and Cahokia bands spoke the same language as those at the north, and by some historians called Illinoisans, but it is a well-known fact that these bands were not engaged in the many wars with the Iroquois before and after the French came to the country, and they took no part in the war that followed the assassination of Pontiac. The Illinois Indians proper, against whom the allies made war, included only those bands living between the Sangamon River and Lake Michigan. It was against these northern bands that the different tribes made war, which terminated in their annihilation, the last of whom perished on Starved Rock, an account of which will be narrated in a subsequent chapter.

AN ERROR OF HISTORY. 143

According to history Pontiac was killed in the fall of 1769, and the traditions of both French and Indians agree that the Starved Rock tragedy occurred in the fall of the same year. All accounts agree that a bloody war intervened between the former and latter events, and this establishes a connecting link between the two. For the purpose of showing that the Indian killed at Cahokia was not Pontiac I give the statement of an old gentleman, still living, who was born and raised where this event occurred, and his statement harmonizes with others.

Auguste Binet says in his boyhood days a party of Indians were in the habit of making almost daily visits to Cahokia for the purpose of trade, drinking whisky, etc. Among these visitors was an old Indian who witnessed the assassination of the reputed Pontiac, and made many statements in relation to it. He said the Indian killed at Cahokia was a petty Ottawa chief from Michigan who is said to have resembled Pontiac both in face and form. This Indian representing himself to be Pontiac had spent some time at St. Vincent, on the Wabash, in trying to raise a force for the purpose of capturing the British garrison at that place. But failing in this he came to St. Louis, and offered his services to Captain St. Ange in retaking of Illinois by enlisting a large band of warriors to capture Fort Chartres, but meeting with no encouragement from the commander he left for Cahokia, where he was assassinated a few days afterward.

The assassin was a drunken, worthless vagabond name Spawse, who suffered the penalty of his crime, being condemned and executed according to law. Williamson, who was accused of being accessory to the murder, sold out his stock-in-trade a few days after the assassination, and fled from the country to escape punishment for his crime.

THE OTTAWAS ORDERED OUT OF THE COUNTRY.

It has already been stated that Pontiac with a remnant of his band established a village on the Kankakee River, and here the great warrior, hero of many battles, intended to end his days in peace and quiet far away from the English, whom he so much hated. But the country of his adoption belonged to the Illinois Indians, who regarded the Ottawas as intruders. Kineboo, the head chief of the Illinoisans, accompanied by a retinue of warriors all mounted on ponies, went to the Ottawa camp, and found the new-comers engaged in building lodges and making preparations to plant corn. The chief notified Pontiac's band that they were trespassers, and gave them two moons to leave the country, and if found there at the expiration of that time he would remove them by force. But when the Illinoisans learned that the Ottawas were backed by the powerful tribe of Pottawatomies they did not molest them.*

MASSACRE OF A HUNTING PARTY.

On account of the green-headed flies the buffalo would leave the Wabash country and range west and north of the Illinois River during the summer months. In the east part of the state buffalo were seldom seen, while the prairie westward for miles in extent was frequently blackened by large herds of them. On this account the Pottawatomies and Ottawas were in the habit of hunting west of the river, which gave offense to the Illinoisans, who regarded it as a trespass on their rights.

A party of about thirty Ottawa hunters, among whom was Pontiac, had been killing buffalo during the day on the prairie eight leagues west of La Vantum. At night the hunters camped in a grove of timber, with the intention of renewing the hunt on the fol-

---

*The above facts relating to Pontiac I obtained from Shaubona, a celebrated chief who was well-known in this part of the country, and whose veracity has never been questioned. Shaubona's father belonged to Pontiac's band, came to Illinois with them, and here at this village on the Kankakee River the old chief was born. Rev. David K. Foster, an educated half-breed now living in Allegan county, Michigan, is a nephew of Shaubona, and has furnished me many items in relation to his grandfather. He says his grandfather was a chief under Pontiac, also engaged in subsequent wars, and one of the signers of the treaty at Greenville in 1795. The speech made at that time by him has been handed down by tradition, of which Foster has written out in full and furnished me with a copy of it.

lowing day. Next morning while the hunters were sitting around a camp-fire unconscious of danger they were attacked by a large party of Illinois warriors, and many of them slain. Pontiac was wounded, but by the swiftness of his pony made good his escape.*

A bloody war followed this massacre, and for a time both parties met with victories and defeats. The Pottawatomies and Ottawas would send war parties into the Illinois country, burn their towns, destroy corn, kill squaws and papooses, and carry off ponies, furs, etc. Then the Illinoisans would retaliate on their enemies by making raids into their country, killing defenseless squaws, burning and destroying everything that lay in their way. After this war had continued for some time the Illinoisans

---

* The grove referred to is supposed to have been the head of Bureau timber, near the village of La Moille, and known in the early settlement of the country as Dimmick Grove. In the spring of 1830 Daniel Dimmick made a claim here, and built a cabin near the head of the grove, on what is now known as the Collins farm. He lived on this claim about two years, until the beginning of the Black Hawk war, when he left it and never returned, but for many years the grove bore his name.

A short distance below Dimmick's cabin, near the bank of Pike Creek, and by the side of a spring, was an old Indian camping-ground, and during the fall and winter hunting parties were frequently found here. In the winter of 1830–31 a party of Indians from the Illinois River, among whom was the noted chief Shick Shack, were encamped here for many days, while hunting deer in the grove.

Shick Shack said to Dimmick, while in conversation, that a long time ago a hunting party of Ottawa Indians were encamped on this very spot, when they were attacked by the Illinoisans, a large portion of them killed, and their great war chief, Pontiac, wounded. From that time, continued the old chief, the tribes were at war with each other, which continued until all the Illinoisans were slain, the last of whom perished on Starved Rock.

sued for peace, and a council was called by the contending parties to agree on terms.

INDIAN COUNCIL. PONTIAC ASSASSINATED.*

A council met at the great mound on the Des Plaines River, near the present site of Joliet, and was attended by all the principal chiefs of the respective tribes. For a time the deliberations of the council were harmonious, but when the allies claimed a part of the Illinois territory as the only condition of peace, ill feelings were manifested. Kineboo, the head chief of the Illinoisans, in a speech said: "Rather than submit to these terms we will sacrifice the last drop of blood in our veins, and leave our squaws and papooses to be tomahawked and scalped by a barbarous enemy." Pontiac next addressed the council, and great attention was given to what he said. His tall, manly form, unimpaired by age, was an object of admiration, and his sprightly eloquence carried all his friends with him. With much enthusiasm he called on his brother chiefs to stand by him, and never lay down the tomahawk until their terms were acceded to. While Pontiac was

* NOTE.—The assassination of Pontiac, the war which followed it, and the tragedy of Starved Rock, are compiled principally from traditionary accounts recently collected among the Pottawatomies and Ottawas of western Kansas, whose ancestors lived on the Illinois River. The accounts given of these events were gathered by Colonel Joseph N. Bournassa, an educated half-breed of Silver Lake Kansas, expressly for this book, and there can be no doubt about the principal facts.

thus speaking Kineboo drew his scalping-knife and stabbed him to the heart. Thus perished the greatest warrior of his day.

Over the remains of Pontiac the warriors held a council, at which it was agreed to avenge his death, and they made preparations for its execution. They cut off the head and legs of the dead chief, boiled them to separate the flesh from the bones, and with the skull and cross-bones placed on a pointed pole they were prepared to go forth to victory. Miamis, Kickapoos, Shawnees, Chippewas, and other tribes who had fought with Pontiac, came forward to avenge his death. Even the white outlaw Bernett, who had long since become a savage and chief of a small band, marshaled his warriors and took a part in the bloody strife. The combined forces of these tribes constituted the most formidable Indian army ever collected in the west, and for savage brutality it has no parallel in the annals of Indian warfare. Their motto was victory or death, no quarter to the enemy, and never lay down the tomahawk until the Illinoisans were annihilated.

A WAR OF EXTERMINATION.

The allied forces attacked and destroyed all the villages along the Illinois River, killing and scalping defenseless squaws and papooses, but the principal town, La Vantum, which was fortified and defended by the bravest warriors, they had not molested. At this town the remnants of the different bands were collected, and here they intended to make their last defense against the victorious invaders. Small timbers and brush were brought from a neighboring grove with which barricades had been erected around three sides of the town the river bounding the fourth. Inside this fortification were collected from many distant towns all that was left of the Illinois Indians, numbering perhaps about ten thousand, of whom two thousand were warriors.

Days and weeks passed away, the summer almost ended, and the enemy had not appeared, and it was thought they had left the country. Preparations were made for holding a great feast, offering up sacrifices to the gods of war for deliverance from their enemies. Music and dancing were again introduced into the great Illinois town, and people old and young gave themselves up to enjoyment as in former days. The warriors brought forth scalps taken from the enemy, and in merry glee danced around them. Naked papooses played in the dirt, running to and fro in their childlike sports. Young maidens and their lovers amused themselves with songs and dances, and talking of happy days in the future. Thus for many days the Indians gave themselves up to feasting and amusements, unconscious of the great calamity which was about to befall them.

It was near the close of a warm day in the early part of Indian summer when the Indians, old and young of both sexes, were arrayed in their best apparel, ornamented with beads, feathers, rings, etc., were collected on an open square to celebrate the marriage of the head chief's daughter. But while in the midst of gaiety they were horrified to see the great meadow to the east covered by the enemy, who were moving on them with great rapidity. In front of the invaders on a red pole was carried the skull and cross-bones of Pontiac, showing that no quarter would be given. The drums beat, warriors grasped their arms and in a moment were ready for battle, while a wail of lamentation was raised by the frightened squaws and papooses. On came the allied forces with such rapidity that a large number of them scaled the breastworks, and entered the town without opposition. But here the assailants were met by the defenders, and most of them slain before they could recross it to join their comrades. When the invaders witnessed the fate of their comrades they were spell-bound, and before recovering from the panic the Illinoisans with a large force attacked them, when in confusion they fled, leaving behind them their dead and wounded.

The invaders, having been repulsed with great slaughter, retired to Buffalo Rock, where a consultation was held, at which they agreed to renew the attack in the morning and continue the fighting until the Illinoisans were exterminated. Morning came, and with it also came blood and carnage unequaled in Indian warfare.

After the invaders were repulsed the victors spent the night in dancing over the scalps, and offering up sacrifices to the Great Manitou for success in battle. Having spent the night in rejoicing they were found asleep in the morning, and while slumbering they were again attacked, and before they could marshal their hosts the invaders in large numbers entered the town, killing all that lay in their way, sparing neither squaws, papooses, aged or infirm. But the assailants were again met by brave warriors, and repulsed with great slaughter. Again and again the town was entered, when a hand-to-hand conflict raged with fearful strife, the allies falling back only for reinforcements. For twelve long hours the battle raged, a large portion of the Illinois warriors were slain, and hundreds of squaws and papooses lay lifeless in their bloody gore. Night at last came, but the battle continued. Against the large invading force the defenders could make but a feeble resistance, and soon all must be slain. But fortunately a heavy rain-storm came on, and in the darkness of the night it became impossible to distinguish friends from foes, consequently for a time further slaughter was suspended.

CHAPTER XIII.

THE ROCK OF REFUGE.

DURING a rain-storm, and in the darkness of the night, the Illinoisans launched their canoes across the river, and ascended Starved Rock. Here on this rock were collected the remnant of the Illinois Indians, consisting of about twelve hundred, three hundred of whom were warriors. On the summit of Starved Rock the fugitives felt secure from their enemies, and they offered up prayers and sang songs of praise to the Great Manitou for their safe deliverance. Many years before, Tonti with fifty French soldiers and one hundred Indian allies held this rock when attacked by two thousand Iroquois warriors, and put them to flight, consequently on this spot they felt secure from their enemies.

Morning came, and with it a clear sky and a bright sun, and from their elevated position they looked down on their enemies encamped on the great meadow below. Soon the allied forces were in motion, moving on the town to complete their bloody work, but soon discovered their intended victims had fled. The wounded, sick, and infirm by age, who could not escape with their friends, were slain, the town burned, and the dead bodies left unburied, where their swollen and distorted remains were found many days afterward.

The allied forces forded the river on the rapids, surrounded Starved Rock, and made preparations to ascend it to complete their victory. With deafening yells the warriors crowded up the steep, rocky pathway, but on reaching the summit they were met by brave Illinoisans, who with war-clubs and tomahawks sent them bleeding and lifeless down the rugged precipice. Again and again the assailants rallied, and rushed forward to assist their friends, but one after another were slain on reaching the summit, and their dead bodies thrown from the rock into the river below. On came fresh bands of assailants. The fearful struggle continued until the rock was red and slippery with human gore, and the yells of the victors could be heard above the shrieks and groans of the dying. Connected with this bloody battle on Starved Rock is a romantic story, which was current at the time among the French and halfbreeds at Peoria, and is now narrated by their descendants. A young warrior named Belix, a halfbreed, who had distinguished himself in previous battles, and wore on his breast a badge of honor, which designated him the bravest of the brave. This young warrior having wooed and won a beautiful maiden, a daughter of the head chief, Kineboo, and the time had arrived to celebrate the marriage rites. But in the midst of the marriage festival, and before the bride was given away, the ceremony was brought to a close by the alarm of approaching enemy, as previously stated. When the allied forces assaulted the fugitives on Starved Rock foremost among the warriors in repelling the assailants was young Belix, and with his war-club cleaved the skulls of many of the enemy. During the fight his fancied bride stood near by witnessing the bloody strife as one after another fell before his magic war-club, but at last saw her lover's skull split open with a tomahawk. With a wild scream she sprang from the rock down the fearful precipice, her body falling from crag to crag until it landed mangled, bleeding and lifeless in the river below.

THE BESIEGERS AND BESIEGED.

On a high, rocky cliff south of Starved Rock, known as Devil's Nose, the allied forces collected during the night small timbers, with which they erected a temporary breastwork. From this breastwork they fired on the besieged, killing some and wounding others, and among the latter was Kineboo, head chief of the tribe. The fortification protecting the south side of Starved Rock had fallen into decay, fifty-one years having elapsed since the French abandoned Fort St. Louis. The palisades had rotted off, and earth-works moulded down to one-half their original height, consequently they afforded but little protection. To remedy the defect the besieged cut down some of the stunted cedars that crowned the summit of the rock, with which they erected barricades along the embankment to shield themselves from the rifle-balls and arrows of the enemy.

The besieged were now protected from the missiles of their assailants, but another enemy still more dreadful—-that of hunger and thirst—began to alarm them. When they took refuge here on the rock they carried with them a small quantity of provision, but this supply was now exhausted, and starvation stared them in the face. At first this rock was thought to be a haven of safety, but it now appeared likely to be their tomb, but without a murmur brave warriors made preparations to meet their fate. Day after day passed away, mornings and evenings came and went, and still the Illinoisans continued to be closely guarded by the enemy, leaving them no opportunity to escape from their rocky prison. Famishing with thirst caused them to cut up some of their buckskin clothing, out of which they made cords to draw water out of the river, but the besiegers had placed a guard at the base of the rock, protected by a projecting crag, and as soon as the vessel reached the water cut the cord, or by giving it a quick jerk pulled the water drawer over the precipice, and his body fall headlong into the river below.

As days passed away the besieged sat on the rock gazing on the great meadow below, over which they had ofttimes roamed at pleasure, and they longed for freedom once more. The site of their town was in plain view, but instead of lodges and camping-tents with people passing to and fro, as in former days, it was now a lonely, dismal waste, blackened by fire, and covered with the swollen and ghastly remains of the slain. Buzzards were hovering around, flying back and forth over the desolated town, and feasting on the dead bodies of their friends. At night they looked upon the silent stars toward the spirit land, and in their wild imagination saw angels waiting to receive them. While sleeping they dreamed of roaming over woods and prairie in pursuit of game, or cantering their ponies across the plains, but on awaking from their slumber they found it all a delusion. Their sleep was disturbed by the moans and sighs of the sufferers, and when morning came it was but the harbinger of another day of torture. From their rocky prison they could see the ripe corn in their fields, and on a distant prairie a herd of buffalo were grazing, but while in sight of plenty of food they were famishing with hunger. Below them at the base of the rock flowed the Illinois River, and as its clear, rippling water glided softly by it appeared in mockery to their burning thirst.

They had been twelve days on the rock, closely guarded by the enemy, much of that time suffering from hunger and thirst. Their small stock of provision had long since become exhausted, and early and late the little ones were heard crying for food. The mother would hold her infant to her breast to soothe its wailing, but alas, the fountain that supported life had dried up, and the little sufferer would turn away with a feeble cry. Young maidens whose comely form, sparkling eyes and blooming cheeks were the pride of the band, became pale, feeble and emaciated, and with a feeling of resignation they looked upward to their home in the spirit land. One of the squaws, the companion of a noted chief, while in a fit of delirium caused by hunger and thirst threw her infant from the summit of the rock into the river below, and with a wild, piercing scream followed it. A few brave warriors attempted to escape from their rocky prison, but on descending were slain by the vigilant guards. Others in their wild frenzy hurled their tomahawks at the fiends below, and singing their death song laid down to die.

The last lingering hope was now abandoned, hunger and thirst had done their dreadful work, the cries of the young, and lamentations of the aged, were heard only in a whisper, their tongues swollen and their lips crisped from thirst so they could scarcely give utterance to their sufferings. Old white-headed chiefs, feeble and emaciated, reduced almost to a skeleton, crept away under branches of evergreens to breathe their last. Proud young warriors preferred to die upon this strange rocky fortress by starvation and thirst rather than surrender themselves to the scalping knives of a victorious enemy. Many had died, their remains lying here and there on the rocky summit, and the effluvium caused by putrefaction greatly annoyed the besiegers. A few of the more hardy warriors for a time feasted on the dead, eating the flesh and drinking the blood of their comrades as soon as life was extinct.

A party of the allied forces now ascended the rock and tomahawked all those who had survived the famine, scalping old and young, and left the remains to decay on the rock, where the bones were seen many years afterward. Thus perished the large tribe of Illinois Indians, and with the exception of a solitary warrior they became extinct.

Near the close of the Starved Rock siege a young warrior during a severe rain-storm and darkness of the night took a buckskin cord, which had been used for drawing water, and fastening it to the trunk of a cedar tree let himself down into the river, and thus made his escape, being the only survivor of this fearful tragedy. This young warrior was partly white, being a descendant, on his father's side, from the French, who lived at Fort St. Louis many years before. Being alone in the world, without friends or kindred, he went to Peoria, joined the colony, and there ended his days. He embraced Christianity, became an officer in the church, assuming the name of Antonia La Bell, and his descendants are now living near Prairie du Rocher, one of whom, Charles La Bell, was a party to a suit in the United States court to recover the land where Peoria now stands.

VARIOUS TRADITIONARY EVIDENCE.

Colonel Joseph N. Bourassa, of Silver Lake, Kansas, who collected from among his people, whose ancestors lived on the Illinois River, a large amount of traditionary matter relating to the massacre on Starved Rock, says no incident in Indian warfare made so lasting an impression on their minds as this, and the main facts relating thereto will be kept in remembrance for many generations to come. The many accounts collected by Colonel Bourassa differ somewhat in detail, but all agree on the principal events — that it occurred in the fall of 1769, and the Illinoisans were all annihilated. Bourassa says when a boy he heard two aged warriors, who had participated in the massacre of Starved Rock, narrate many incidents which took place at the time, and this account corresponds with other stories that have come down through several generations.

In the early settlement of the country an old Indian named Mashaw frequently visited the tradinghouses at Hennepin and Ottawa, and through an interpreter made various statements in relation to the Starved Rock tragedy. He said at the time it occurred he was a small boy, accompanying his father; was present at the siege, and saw the destruction of the Illinois Indians. He said after many days' fighting a number of warriors during the night descended from the rock, and attempted to fight their way through the lines, but were all slain except seven, who succeeded in effecting their liberty.

As late as 1828 a small band of Indians had a village on the north side of Lake Depue, and raised corn on a little bottom prairie now included in the farm of Charles Savage. Among these Indians was a very old man, who frequently accompanied his grandson in a canoe to Hartzell's trading house near the present site of Hennepin. This old Indian said he was born on the Wabash, and was ten years old at the time of the Starved Rock tragedy. His father participated in this affair, and two of his uncles were killed in the fight before the Illinoisans took refuge on the rock. He said the fight at the town lasted two days, and hundreds of warriors on both sides were slain. Two years after this affair the band to which this old Indian belonged emigrated to Illinois, and built a town on the south side of the river opposite Lake Depue. At that time, and for many years after, where the great battle was fought acres of ground were covered with human bones, and the summit of Starved Rock almost covered with skulls and bones of the victims. Medore Jennette, an employé of Auguste and Pietre Chouteau, fur-traders at St. Louis, lived many years in an Indian village at the mouth of the Fox River, and has left his numerous descendants many traditions relating to early times. Jennette came to the country in 1772, three years after the Illinois Indians were annihilated, and found the summit of Starved Rock covered with human bones. The Indians believed an evil spirit stood guard over these bones, and on account of this superstitious notion they could not be prevailed on to go near the rock.

A short distance below Starved Rock, on what

was then known as the great battle-field, many acres of ground were whitened by bones and skulls.

An old Indian called Shaddy, who was born and raised on the Illinois River, went west with his band in 1834. Two years afterward he came back to look once more upon the scenes of his youth, and during the winter of 1836-7 hunted in the river timber and along Bureau Creek. In conversation with this old Indian I obtained many interesting items in relation to past events. He said his father was at the siege of Starved Rock, and all the Illinois Indians perished except one. This was a young half-breed who let himself down into the river by a buck-skin cord during a severe rain-storm, and in the darkness of the night made his escape.

A GHASTLY SPECTACLE.

A few days after the destruction of the Illinois Indians a party of traders from Peoria, among whom were Robert Maillet and Felix La Pance, while returning from Canada with three canoes loaded with goods, stopped at the scene of the late tragedy. On approaching Starved Rock they noticed a cloud of buzzards hovering over it, and at the same time were greeted with a sickening odor. On landing from their canoes and ascending the rock they found the steep, rugged pathway leading thereto stained with blood, and among the stunted cedars that grew on the cliff were a number of human bodies partly devoured by birds of prey. But on reaching the summit they were horrified to find it covered with dead bodies, all in an advanced state of decomposition. Here was the aged chief with silver locks, lying by the side of young warriors whose long raven hair partly concealed their ghastly and distorted features. Here, too, were squaws and papooses, the aged grandmother, and the young maiden, with here and there an infant still clasped in its mother's arms. Some had died from thirst and starvation, others by the tomahawk or war club; of the latter their remains were partly enveloped in a pool of clotted blood. All the dead, without regard to age or sex, had been scalped, and the remains divested of clothing.

The swollen and distorted remains of the slain were hideous to look upon, and the stench from them so offensive that the traders hastened down from the rock, and continued on their way down the river.

On reaching La Vantum, a short distance below Starved Rock, the traders met with a still greater surprise, and for a time were almost ready to believe what they saw was delusion instead of reality. The great town of the west had disappeared; not a lodge, camping-tent, or one human being, could be seen. All was desolate, silent and lonely. The ground where the town had stood was strewn with dead bodies, and packs of hungry wolves were feeding upon their hideous repast.

Five months before these traders while on their way to Canada stopped at La Vantum, for the purpose of trading with the Indians. At that time the inhabitants, about five thousand in number, were in full enjoyment of life, but now their dead bodies lay mouldering on the ground, food for wolves and birds of prey. The traders had bought of these people two canoe loads of furs and pelts, which were to be paid for in goods on their return from Canada. The goods were now here to make payment according to contract, but alas, the creditors had all gone to their long home.

The smell from hundreds of putrefied remains was so offensive that the traders remained only a short time, and with sadness they turned away from this scene of horror. The traders again boarding their canoes passed down the river to Peoria, conveying thither to their friends the sad tidings.

CHAPTER XIV.

RELICS OF THE TRAGEDY.

IN the following spring, after the Illinois Indians were annihilated, a party of traders from Cahokia on their way to Canada, in canoes loaded with furs, stopped at Peoria. On reaching this point they heard of the destruction of the Indians on Starved Rock, and were afraid to proceed further on their journey. After remaining a few days at Peoria they proceeded on their way, accompanied as far as Starved Rock by twenty-one Frenchmen and a number of Indians. With this escort was Father Buche, a Jesuit priest of Peoria, and an account of his observations are preserved in his manuscript.*

When the voyageurs arrived at La Vantum they found the town site strewed with human bones, and fragments of broken pottery, and a few charred poles alone marked the location of the great town of the west. Scattered over the prairie were hundreds of skulls, some of which still retained a portion of flesh, and partly covered with long black hair, giving to

*An account of this manuscript will be found in the succeeding chapter, and from which many extracts have been taken.

the remains a ghastly and sickening appearance. This party also ascended Starved Rock, and found its summit covered with bones and skulls, among masses of putrefied flesh. Here among the remains of the dead were found knives, tomahawks, rings, beads, and various trinkets, some of which the travelers carried with them to Canada, and can now be seen among the antiquarian collection in Quebec.

Various accounts are given in after years both by French and Indians of seeing relics of this fearful tragedy on the summit of Starved Rock. Pierre Bulbona, an Indian trader known by many of the early settlers, said when a small boy he accompanied his father in ascending Starved Rock, and saw many relics of the slaughtered Indians. This was only fifteen years after the massacre, and the rock was covered with skulls and bones, all in a good state of preservation, but bleached white by the sun and rain. Persons are still living among the French fur traders who have seen these bones on the summit of Starved Rock, and at the present time small fragments of human remains are occasionally found. On my first visit to Starved Rock, forty-five years ago, I found a number of human teeth, and small fragments of bones. Some years ago a human skull was found at the root of a tree, buried up with leaves and dirt, also a tomahawk and a large scalping knife. At different times visitors have found relics of the past, consisting of weapons of war and trinkets of various kinds, and still retain them as trophies of the past.

Whoever will take the trouble to examine the soil on Starved Rock will find in many places a peculiar dusty sediment among the dirt, showing decomposed animal matter, which, without doubt, is the remains of human beings. I have visited the catacombs belonging to different Italian cities, also those around Jerusalem, and walked over the dust made from the remains of human beings, and find the sediment among the dirt on Starved Rock to be of the same kind.

SEARCHING FOR GOLD.

When the Governor of Canada took possession of Fort St. Louis all the goods, furs, etc., belonging to the traders were confiscated to the government, and report says divided between the governor and friends. Tonti having in his possession at that time a large sum of gold dug a pit hole within the stockades and buried it, to prevent its falling into the hands of his enemies. Sixteen years afterward, as Tonti was about to die, he told a priest, who was holding a gold cross before his face, about the gold being buried within the fort. The priest kept this matter a secret, waiting for an opportunity to resurrect the gold, but was drowned soon after by the upsetting of a canoe. A short time after the death of the priest the fort was burned by the Indians, and the French driven away, as previously stated.

In the summer of 1765, forty-seven years after the burning of Fort St. Louis, a party of French at Peoria, among whom were Captain M. De Fond and Father Buche, believing the story about gold being buried in the fort came up the river in search of it. This party of gold hunters encamped at the base of Starved Rock, and spent some days in digging holes on its summit, which accounts for the many pit holes now to be seen. No gold was found by these adventurers, but in a vault near where the store-house stood they found a large number of tomahawks, guns, knives, beads, and various kinds of trinkets, intended for the Indian trade.

An account of searching for gold on the summit of Starved Rock is given in Father Buche's manuscript, in which he says: "We had spent five days in digging holes on the top of Le Rocher, and found a large quantity of articles which were intended for the Indian trade, but of the precious metal, the object of our search, we found none. On the last day of our stay we dug a large hole close to the old earthworks, and continued at work until it was quite dark, when the devil appeared to us in the form of a huge bear. On seeing this monster we dropped our tools, and hurried down from Le Rocher, put our camp kit in a canoe, and started down the river for home."

In the summer of 1805 a party of adventurers at Kaskaskia learning from tradition that a large amount of gold had been buried within the stockades of Fort St. Louis went in search of it. At that time the location of the old fort was unknown; history and tradition alike failed to point it out, but they knew it was on a high rock washed by the rapid current of the Illinois. and a short distance above the great bend in the river. On Buffalo Rock they found what they believed to be the relics of Fort St. Louis, and here they spent many days in searching for the hidden treasures, but finding none they returned home. An account of this expedition was published in the newspapers of that day, which describe the remains of the fort on a large rock on the north side of the river, and from that time it was believed that Fort St. Louis had been built on Buffalo Rock.

The story of gold having been buried within the stockades of Fort St. Louis is also among the Indian traditions, and some years ago a party of Pottawatomies came from Kansas in search of it. People in the vicinity told them that the fort had stood on Buffalo Rock, and on its summit they dug many pit holes, but finding none of the precious metal they returned to their homes in the west.

FORT ST. LOUIS, ROCK FORT, AND LE ROCHER.

In former times people of the west generally believed that Fort St. Louis was built on Buffalo Rock, as relics of an ancient fortification were found here in the early settlement of the country. But in comparing the various historical accounts, as well as French and Indian traditions, it is shown conclusively to have stood on Starved Rock, and here its remains can still be seen. Buffalo Rock does not answer the description of the place spoken of in history, and the natural advantages between it and Starved Rock for a fort could not escape the observation of a man with La Salle's shrewdness. Buffalo Rock contains on its summit several hundred acres, is only about sixty feet high, whereas Starved Rock is one hundred and thirty-six feet high, containing less than one acre on its summit, and accessible only at one place. Thus it is a natural fortress, where but little labor would be required to make it impregnable, so a few soldiers could hold it against all the savages of the west. Fort St. Louis, Rock Fort and Le Rocher, so often referred to in history, are without doubt all one and the same place.

South of Starved Rock, about one hundred and fifty yards distant, is a high knoll, isolated from the neighboring bluff, covered with scattering trees, and known in early times as Devil's Nose.*

Eastward across a chasm two hundred yards wide is a rocky cliff as high as Starved Rock and covered with stunted evergreens. This cliff rises almost perpendicular from the water's edge, connects with the main bluff, and from an old Indian legend is called Maiden's Leap.†

These two cliffs are within gun-shot of the fort, therefore it became necessary to protect the side of the rock next to them with earth-works and palisade.

A more romantic place for building a fort could not be found in the western country, and for natural defenses or picturesque appearance it is without a parallel in history. The many remarkable events connected with this old relic of antiquity if given to the world would rival the works of fiction, surpassing even the wild romance of feudal times.

The river at this point assumes a different character, no longer a dull, sluggish stream, but is wide, shallow and rapid, and its broad channel divided by

---

* For many years after the Starved Rock tragedy a superstitious notion prevailed among the Indians, who believed that an evil spirit had taken possession of this eminence, and every night when the winds blew and rain fell he could be heard blowing his nose.

† It is said a young and beautiful Indian maiden, a daughter of a noted chief, having been crossed in love jumped off this cliff, and her mangled body was found in the ravine below some days afterward.

many beautiful wood-clad islands. Some of these islands are now under cultivation, while others are covered with forest trees, the tall cottonwood and outspreading elms adding beauty and romance to the surrounding scenery.

These islands in the river, with the land on which Starved Rock stands, belong to Colonel D. F. Hitt, of Ottawa, who entered it nearly half a century ago.

RELICS OF FORT ST. LOUIS.

In the summer of 1721, thirty-nine years after Fort St. Louis was built, Charlevoix, a French Jesuit priest, visited Illinois, and in his journal gave some account of the scenery along the river. On Buffalo Rock he found an Indian village surrounded by a rude fortification, consisting of low earth-works with stockades, and known as Le Fort des Miamis. About one league below Buffalo Rock, on the opposite side of the river, is Le Rocher, rising from the water's edge like a castle wall, to the height of one hundred and fifty feet, and can be ascended only at one point. On this rock, says Charlevoix, La Salle built a fort, and part of the palisade was still standing. The block-house, store-house and dwellings had been burned by the Indians, and everything about the fort was in ruins, although it had been occupied by his countrymen only three years before.

The remains of earth-works can still be seen, encircling about two-thirds of the rock, and following around it on the brink of the precipice. These works commence on the western angle, following the margin of the rock to the extreme eastern curve, leaving an open gateway at the place of ascending the rock, and are one hundred and twenty-two yards in length. On the south side of the rock, along these earth-works, are many pit holes, two of which are very large, and in all probability one of these was the magazine, and the other a cellar of a storehouse. The smaller pit holes which are found here and there among the evergreens, according to Buche's manuscript, were dug forty-seven years after the destruction of the fort, by persons while searching for gold.

INDIAN AND FRENCH RELICS.

In the vicinity of Starved Rock, and near the site of the old Indian village, many relics have been found, consisting of gun flints, arrow-heads, etc. Earthen pots, kettles, and various kinds of pottery, have been found, also tomahawks, axes, knives, hoes, with various kinds of farming and war implements made of stone. Burton Ayres, one of the pioneers of La Salle, collected many curious relics of Indian antiquities, among which was an image in the form of a man cut out of limestone, and supposed to have been an idol of heathen worship. On the site of La-Vantum many curious relics have been found, and every year in plowing the ground new trinkets are discovered. People living in that locality have collected a large amount of Indian relics, some of which have been placed in the Ottawa Academy of Natural Science for preservation.

On and around Starved Rock many relics of the early French occupants have also been found, consisting of farming implements of European manufacture, rifle and cannon balls, gold and silver crosses, with various trinkets of more or less value. A few years ago a small cannon was found imbedded in the river bank, where it had lain perhaps for nearly two centuries. This cannon is made of wrought iron, hooped with heavy rings to make it strong like those used in Europe centuries ago. This ancient piece of ordnance in all probability was brought from Canada by La Salle or some of his men to be used on a fortification, and may have been the one mounted on the ramparts of Fort St. Louis at the time of its dedication, and fired a salute in honor of the King of France.

A short time ago an old cedar tree was cut down on the summit of Starved Rock, and within its trunk was found imbedded a gun barrel partly destroyed by rust. How this gun barrel came here will forever remain a mystery, but in all probability it was the work of an ingenious Frenchman, during the occupation of Fort St. Louis. This gun barrel, with a portion of the tree which surrounded it, also the old cannon found in the river bank, with many other curiosities, are preserved among the collection of relics at Ottawa Museum of Natural Science.

A short time ago David Walker, of Ottawa, found near Buffalo Rock a piece of copper about the size and shape of a half dollar, on which was engraved in rude characters the name of Tonti. It is quite probable this trinket is one among the many medals which the commander of Fort St. Louis distributed among his Indian friends as a token of remembrance.

On Starved Rock were found two bronze medallion heads of noted persons of those days, one of King Louis XIV and the other of Pope Leo X.

Colonel D. F. Hitt, of Ottawa, has now in his possession a double cross made of pure gold, three inches in length, but without name or date. This cross is said to be an insignia of an Archbishop, and was probably lost by one of the holy fathers who frequented Fort St. Louis.

This cross was found seven years ago, about two hundred feet west of Starved Rock, and an account of its size and engraving has attracted much attention. On one side of this emblem are four hearts and four open links, with a human figure representing Christ nailed to the cross. On the opposite side are six hearts and four links, with an image of the Virgin Mary holding the infant Christ in her arms. The figures and images on this cross are well engraved, being of the same style of work as those ancient Christian emblems now on exhibition in the Vatican, at Rome.

It has been a matter of much speculation how a cross representing this high order in the Catholic church came to Fort St. Louis, as no one higher than a priest had officiated as chaplain during thirty-six years of its occupation. There is an incident connected with the fort which may throw some light on it, and were all the facts known might possibly explain this mystery. The Archbishop of Rouen sent to Canada a fine satin robe, a large gold cross, with other sacred emblems, to be presented to the most devoted priest in North America. The priests at Quebec awarded these gifts to Father Chrisp, chaplain of Fort St. Louis, but he died before their arrival, and in the fall of 1688 these things were presented to Father Caudier, brother of La Salle. It is possible that the cross found here may be the one referred to, and lost by the owner during his rambles around the fort.

Colonel Hitt has two other crosses which were found in the vicinity of Starved Rock, but they are of the kind usually worn by priests and monks, and do not differ materially from those found elsewhere.

In the vicinity of Starved Rock are found many under-ground furnaces consisting of a large flue built of stone and mortar. The French in those days were in the habit of building flues under their dwellings to warm them, and this manner of warming a house is still in use in some parts of Canada.

FATHER BUCHE'S MANUSCRIPT.

This old manuscript, now in the hands of Hypolite Pilette, consists of twenty-three pages closely written on large sheets, and from age the paper is yellow and ink faded. It is in the French language, dated at La Ville de Maillet (now Peoria), April 1770, and was written by Jacques Buche, a Jesuit priest. The writer speaks only of things that came under his own observation, and relates a number of remarkable incidents, which are worth preserving. The manuscript speaks of the destruction of La Vantum, the perishing of the remnant of the Illinois Indians on Starved Rock, and from its pages are taken a number of incidents narrated in this book. It also gives an account of digging for gold within the stockades of Fort St. Louis, the pit holes of which can still be seen.

Father Buche speaks of visiting an Indian village fifteen leagues north of La Ville de Maillet, where he remained many days teaching the people the ways of Christianity. The inhabitants of this village said he was possessed of the devil, indulging in vile practices, and idolatrous worship. The chiefs had many wives, and put them to death if they proved barren At their religious feast an infant was burned on the altar as a sacrifice to the Great Manitou, in order that the band might be successful in war hunting, etc., and be protected from the power of the evil one.

Father Buche said he preached many times to these benighted people, and many of them were converted, their names enrolled in the church book, and their souls saved from perdition. He also speaks of accompanying a large party of hunters in slaughtering buffalo, having been run over by the herd, and trampled under the feet of the beasts, but saved from death by the interposition of the Holy Virgin.

CHAPTER XV.

OLD FORT CHARTRES.

THIS old landmark of former times was located near the Mississippi River, and in the northwest corner of Randolph county. The fort was built by the Louisiana company in 1719, and continued to be the seat of government as long as the French were in possession of Illinois. It stood about one-half mile from the river, but connected with it by a slough or bayou, through which boats passed to and from the fort. It was originally a wooden structure, but in 1756 a stone one with high thick walls, containing towers and bastions, took its place. The walls enclosed about four acres of ground, and within this arena were many large buildings for officers and soldiers' quarters. This fort was built of faced blocks of limestone, brought from a cliff on the opposite side of the river, three miles above, and the structure is said to have made a very fine appearance.

Fort Chartres at the time of its construction was considered the most imposing fortification in North America, and over its battlements waved both the

French and British flags. A village of about forty houses, called St. Anne de Fort Chartres, sprang up around the fort, and here was not only the seat of government for Illinois, but it became the center of wealth, business, fashion and gayety.

During the great flood of 1772 a portion of the wall, about one hundred feet in length, was undermined and fell into the river. In consequence of this breach in the walls Fort Chartres was abandoned and went to ruin, the seat of government moved to Kaskaskia, and the inhabitants of the village of St Anne left for other places. A small portion of the walls is still standing, and the magazine remains whole, excepting that a part of the main arch has given way and the great iron door is gone. The foundation and part of the walls of two buildings are standing, with forest trees growing within the enclosure. Most of the large hewed stones of which the main walls were constructed have been taken away to build up towns along the river, and the massive stone arches that encircled the door and gateways now ornament public buildings elsewhere.

These grand old ruins are now in the midst of a forest, with trees more than three feet in diameter standing within their walls; and were the origin of these relics of former times unknown, it might furnish a theme for antiquarian speculation.

In 1788 Congress reserved a tract of land one mile square around Fort Chartres, and this reservation came into market in 1849, and sold the same as other government lands.

FORT MASSAC.

This old landmark of early times was located on the north bank of the Ohio, then called Ouabache River by the French, thirty-six miles from its mouth. The time of its construction is mixed with uncertainty; both history and tradition are alike defective on this point, but it is generally believed to have been built about the year 1711. This fort was built by early French explorers, who came from the lakes by way of Maumee and Wabash rivers, and had no connection with the colonies on the Mississippi.

A short time after the French built this fort it was captured by the Indians through a curious piece of strategy. One day a number of Indians appeared on the opposite side of the river, each covered with a bear skin, walking on all-fours, and imitating the motion of that animal. The soldiers mistook these Indians for bears, and many of them crossed the river in pursuit, while others left their quarters to see the sport. In the meantime a large body of warriors, who were secreted in the woods near by, took possession of the fort without opposition, and but few of the soldiers escaped massacre.

Some years after this tragical affair a new fort was built on the same site, and called Massac in memory of this sad event. This fort was abandoned by the French about the year 1750, but after the close of the revolutionary war the Americans had a garrison here for a short time.

Forty miles above Fort Massac, on the river bank, now in Hardin county, is a place of much note called Cave in the Rock, consisting of a large, romantic-looking cavern at the base of a rocky cliff. For several years this cave was occupied by a band of robbers headed by one Mason. These robbers waylaid boats going to and from New Orleans, murdering the crew and confiscating the cargo. In 1797 this band of outlaws was broken up, some of them captured and executed, while others fled the country to escape punishment.

AMERICAN BOTTOM.

This section of country, so ofttimes referred to by the early western historian, lies on the east side of the Mississippi, extending from Alton to the mouth of Kaskaskia River, a distance of about seventy miles in length, and from three to eight miles in width. This tract of land consists of timber and prairie about equally divided, and much of it subject to inundation, but for fertility of soil it probably is unequaled in the western country. During the first century of the French occupation of Illinois the only permanent settlement (except Peoria) was made on this bottom, and here the descendants of the early pioneers continue to live. The old towns on this bottom still remain French in language, customs and habits, and the people have but little intercourse with those speaking the English language.

The name American Bottom had its origin about a century ago, at the time Illinois came under United States jurisdiction, and from the following circumstance: the west side of the river being known as Louisiana, or New Spain, while on the east, in the river bottom, was called America — hence American Bottom, which name it continues to bear.

In the early settlement of the country the valley of the Mississippi from the Gulf of Mexico to the lakes was known as Louisiana, designated as upper and lower country. In after years the settlements on both sides of the Mississippi were known as the Illinois country, and the same laws were in force, it being one country. After the west side was ceded to Spain it became known as Louisiana, and the territory assumed the name of Missouri about the year 1810, five years after it was ceded to the United States.

PRAIRIE DU ROCHER.

The old French village of Prairie du Rocher is located at the foot of the bluff, three miles from the Mississippi River, and in the northwest corner of Randolph county. There is a rocky cliff, thirty miles long and about two hundred feet high, bounding a fertile bottom, which gives to the place a romantic and picturesque appearance. Its secluded situation, fine scenery, rich soil and large spring of gushing water attracted the attention of early pioneers, and caused it to become a place of importance. A short distance above the town, at the base of a rocky cliff, is a large spring, sending forth an immense volume of water, whose crystal purity might have been taken for the fountain of life, which gave immortality to youth and vigor, so much sought after by the early Spanish explorers. Near this spring is a remarkable cave in the high rocky cliff, but it has never been explored to any great extent, as its chambers are filled with foul air, which is thought to be destructive to life.

According to Jesuit history Prairie du Rocher was incorporated into a village in the year 1722, and a large tract of land granted to its citizens, with an additional tract bounding the Mississippi River for a number of miles for school purposes.

The old Jesuit chapel of St. Joseph, built in 1734,

is still standing, and is probably the oldest building on the American Bottom. Within its portals have been christened the infants of four succeeding generations, and the marriage vows of the people of Prairie du Rocher have been heard at its sacred altar for a century and a half. The register of the chapel, commencing in 1734, containing a record of births, marriages, deaths, etc., was taken to Kaskaskia in 1855 for the purpose of being copied, and, unfortunately, was lost.

CAHOKIA.

When La Salle and his comrades returned from an excursion to the mouth of the Mississippi River in the summer of 1682 they stopped some days at Cahokia, which at that time was a large Indian village. Two Jesuit priests, Pinet and Garvier, who accompanied the expedition, remained here for the purpose of converting the natives. These priests built a chapel in the midst of the village, dedicating it to St. Peter, and named the mission Notre Dame des Cahokia. In the following year La Salle authorized Richard Bosley to establish a trading-post here, and with the traders came many emigrants from Canada, forming the first permanent settlement in the Mississippi Valley. The emigrants built houses in the town with the Indians, and for more than a century they lived together in peace and harmony as one people. Marriage between the French and Indians being legalized by the Catholic church many of the fur traders and early explorers of the west found wives among the blooming daughters of Illinois. Some of the present inhabitants of Cahokia can trace their genealogy back to the time of La Salle, and, their ancestors having intermarried with natives, show strong marks of Indian lineage.

The location of Cahokia is unfavorable for commerce, being situated on Cahokia Creek, a mile and a half from the Mississippi, but still not out of the reach of its floods. In early times the water in the creek was sufficient to float their small crafts, but a Frenchman in seeking revenge cut a channel from the creek into the river, three miles above the town, leaving it without water communication except in time of floods. Along Cahokia Creek are a number of small lakes, and no less than sixty-seven mounds of various sizes and shapes.

Cahokia at the present time is only a small town, the houses standing here and there among gardens and shade trees, the inhabitants mostly engaged in farming, and but few of them can speak or understand English.

KASKASKIA.

According to the most reliable traditionary accounts Father Allouez established a mission at Kaskaskia in 1686, and built a chapel in the Indian village. He gave this mission the sacred name of Immaculate Conception of the Holy Virgin, and its register from 1695 is still preserved among the church papers of the parish. Emigrants from Canada, with fur traders, came to Kaskaskia, and in a few years it became a place of great importance. The congregation continued to occupy the Jesuit chapel until 1721, when a permanent church was built, and occupied as a place of worship for nearly a century. The bell now hanging on the large brick church was brought from France and placed on this building, being the first to ring for public worship in the Mississippi Valley. Its measured strokes have tolled for marriages and funerals of three successive generations, and still the bluff and tall timber around the old town continues to echo its musical peals.

In 1736 a fort was built at Kaskaskia, but never occupied by troops, and burned down after standing thirty-six years. When Fort Chartres was abandoned, in 1772, the government built a new one here called Fort Gage, in honor of the commander-in-chief of the British forces in America, and the relics of this fort can still be seen on the bluff near the river.

After Clark's conquest of Illinois, American emigrants came to Kaskaskia, it being the seat of government for the territory, and also for the state, for about fifty years. People coming to the country made this a place of stopping until a location could be selected elsewhere, and for many years it was the largest and most important town west of the Alleghany mountains; but owing to many floods in the Mississippi River its greatness has long since departed, and at present it is only a small town of but little importance.

KASKASKIA AND CAHOKIA INDIANS.

The Kaskaskia and Cahokia Indians when the French came to the country lived in the towns that bore their respective names, but they had other villages on the American Bottom. These Indians lived on friendly terms with the early settlers, and it was the boast of one of their noted chiefs, Ducogna, that his people had never shed the blood of a white man.

After the northern bands of the Illinois Indians were annihilated their country came into the possession of the victors, consisting of Pottawatomies, Ottawas, Chippewas and Kickapoos. These tribes made war on the Kaskaskia and Cahokia bands, and a number of bloody battles were fought between the contending parties. The hunting-grounds lying between these tribes, including a large portion of the central division of the state, became overrun with game, and for many years neither party would risk hunting here, as they were liable to be attacked by the enemy. In 1782 a battle was fought between these tribes on Battle Ground Creek, twenty-five miles east of Kaskaskia, and for many years the ground of this battle-field was covered with human bones. Another battle between these Indians was fought about the same time on Cache River, now in Johnson county, and the bones of the slain can still be seen in a cave near the battle-ground.

As late as the year 1809 the Kaskaskia Indians had a village of about eight hundred inhabitants, near Prarie du Rocher, and one nearly as large on the Kaskaskia River. At that time the Cahokia Indians had two small villages near their old town, but their number is not known.

There was a band of Kaskaskia Indians at one time on Cache River, known as the wild band, who were engaged in some of the border wars, and were a party to Wayne's treaty at Greenville in 1795, and received annuity from the government. A large portion of this band fell victims to the Kickapoos during one of their raids, and in order to be protected by the whites they left their former home on Cache River and lived in a village near Prairie du Rocher.

The Kaskaskia and Cahokia Indians claimed all

the land in the state south of a line from the mouth of the Illinois River to a point on the Wabash near the present site of Terre Haute. These lands were ceded to the government at a treaty at Edwardsville on September 25, 1818, for a small amount of money, payable annually for twelve years. As the country settled up game became scarce. These Indians went west at different times, the last of them leaving the country in 1833, and a remnant of these bands are now living in the Indian territory south of Kansas.

PEORIA INDIANS.

Indian history is always more or less conflicting, and not very reliable, as each writer on this subject arranges things in accordance to his own fancy. It is an account of people who left no history, and all that is known of them are scraps of tradition, which are more or less veiled in doubt and uncertainty, therefore due allowance should be made for conflicting statements. For more than forty years my attention has been directed to this subject, and statements here given are the result of long investigations.

The principal village of the Peoria Indians was on the west side of Peoria Lake, and called Opa by the French. On La Salle's first visit to this town Neconope was head chief, who is represented as being unfriendly to the whites. But in after years this chief was succeeded by one named Kolet, who became a Christian, and through his influence Jesuits established a mission in his village. French traders built houses in the village, and for more than fifty years whites lived with the Indians. It is said the Peorias had other villages in the vicinity of the lake, but their exact location is unknown.

The Peoria Indians were engaged in the war against the allied forces in defense of their country, and most of the warriors were slain at La Vantum or perished on the summit of Starved Rock. When those at home, being mostly infirm from age, squaws, papooses, etc., heard of the slaughter of their friends they fled to the south to escape a like fate. A few who had intermarried with the French remained at the village and were not molested.

A remnant of a band of Peoria Indians lived at a village south of Cahokia for many years, and were a party to the treaty at Edwardsville on the 25th of September, 1818. At this treaty they sold their land to the government, except a small reservation, and received as consideration two thousand dollars in goods, with an annuity of three dollars for twelve years. Some years after disposing of their lands they sold the reservation, went west of the Mississippi, and mingled with other tribes.

CHAPTER XVI.

INDIAN TRIBES IN ILLINOIS TERRITORY.

AFTER the Illinois Indians were annihilated, in 1769, the conquerors took possession of the country, and occupied it about seventy years. The Illinois River had long been known as the Indian country, being more densely inhabited by them than any other part of the west. Here lived the larger portion of the Illinoisans, and here, too, were found their successors, the Pottawatomies. Between Peoria Lake and the mouth of Fox River were eight Indian villages, some of which were very large, containing hundreds of inhabitants. Although their villages and cornfields were mostly located on or near the Illinois River they claimed as hunting-ground the country between the Wabash and Mississippi Rivers, and over this vast tract they roamed in pursuit of game.

In the year 1800 the commissioner of Indian affairs estimated that thirty thousand Indians, including all the different tribes, were living within the limits of this state, and about three-fifths of this number were on the Illinois River.

In the central portion of the state, on the Mackinaw and Sangamon Rivers, were a few villages of Kickapoo Indians. On the Kankakee River were two villages of Ottawas, and near Lake Michigan were a few villages of Chippeways. Near Rock Island the Sacs and Foxes had two villages, and also one on the present site of Quincy. In the north part of the state were Winnebagoes, and at the south were Kaskaskia and Cahokia Indians.

These Indians at various treaties sold their lands to the government for homes in the west, and left the country at different periods from 1825 to 1836.

MONKS OF LA TRAPPE.

This curious order of religious enthusiasts had its origin in 1664 through a wealthy nobleman named Abbe Rance, who lived in the south of France. For many years he lived a gay, fast life, but on the death of his mistress, Madame Monblazan, he renounced the world, rejected all the comforts of life,— bread and water was his food, and a stone his bed. Rance used his fortune in establishing the order, and had many followers. He built a monastery at La Trappe, and from this fact the name of the order originated.

In the year 1704 about twenty monks of the order

of La Trappe came to Illinois and established themselves on the American Bottom, in St. Clair county. Colonel N. Jerret, of Cahokia, gave them a farm, and furnished money to erect buildings thereon. They built a monastery on the top of a high mound, now known as Monk Hill, and cultivated a small farm near by. Some of the Monks repaired watches, others traded with the people, selling them various kinds of articles, which they brought from France.

These monks were filthy in their habits, very rigid in penance, spending three hours each day in religious exercise, when their songs of praise could be heard far away. The climate did not agree with them; two of the priests and five lay brethren died. They became very unpopular among the people in that locality, and in 1813 they sold their property and returned to France.

OLD FORT NEAR STARVED ROCK.

On the river-bluff, one half-mile south of Starved Rock, are the remains of an ancient fortification, known as the Old Fort, and consist of low, irregular earthworks. This relic of antiquity is located on level land at the intersection of two ravines, and on two sides follows the curve of the hill above the ravines in zigzag lines, with an open gateway at the east, fronting the prairie. These lines enclose about one acre of ground, which is of an oblong shape, and is now covered with large burr-oak trees. This appears to have been only a temporary fortification, consisting of an embankment with a ditch on the inside, and perhaps enclosed with palisades. There are many large trees growing on the embankment and in the ditch, which is conclusive evidence of its great antiquity. Most all the relics of past ages are found in favorable localities, where beauty and convenience have been consulted, but this one appears to be an exception to this rule, and it is a mystery to me why any people would build a fort in such a place as this.

At what time this fort was built, by whom, and for what purpose, will in all probability forever remain a mystery. It could not have been built by the French, for it shows no sign of civil engineering, and neither history nor tradition gives any account of it. Some people believe it was built by the French while in possession of Fort St. Louis, and used as a summer fort to protect themselves from the Indians while raising a crop on the adjoining prairie, but this is not probable, as they always lived on friendly terms with the natives, and therefore needed no protection. Jacques Mette and Hypolite Pilette inform me that their ancestors lived at Fort St. Louis, the former a soldier and the latter a trader, and are positive that no out fortification could have been built by the French without constituting a part of their family traditions. This fort in all probability is the work of people who possessed the country many centuries ago, known as Mound Builders, as many similar relics are found elsewhere.

About two hundred yards northeast of the old fort, by the side of a small ravine, is a shaft of coal near the surface, only a few feet under ground. On examining this shaft a few years ago it was found that the coal had been taken out for some distance, and the embankment on each side of it, made by throwing out the dirt over the coal, is now covered with trees. This work must have been done many centuries ago, and most probably by the occupants of the old fort near by.

THE RUINED CITY OF AZTALAN.

Ancient mounds, low earthworks, and fortifications are found in various localities, but are more common in a favorable place for residence along large streams or on fertile plains, showing that the ancient as well as modern inhabitants were attracted to localities of beauty and convenience. On the bank of Rock River, where the stream expands into a beautiful little lake, causing many natural attractions, are found the remarkable remains of earthworks, known as the ruined city of Aztalan. The ruins of this ancient city were discovered in 1836, and surveyed 'the following year by N. F. Hyer. At that time it attracted much attention, and many extravagant stories were in circulation about its brick walls and stone arches, etc., all of which there is but little truth in.

These works consist of irregular embankments, twenty feet wide on the top, and from three to eight feet high, and one hundred and sixty-six rods in length, forming three sides of an enclosure, the river the fourth, and encircle an area of seventeen and two-thirds acres. At short intervals are buttresses, fifty feet in diameter, composed of red clay of a peculiar mixture, which originated the popular belief that they had been built with brick, and moulded into clay, as we now see it. On the southwest corner of these earthworks is a mound, rising like a pyramid, fifty feet wide at the top, and ascended by a succession of steps. This is supposed to have been the most sacred spot, as well as the highest, and probably contained a temple on its summit. In the northeast corner of the enclosure is another pyramidal elevation, surrounded by rings of small ones supposed to have been mud houses for dwellings or other unknown purposes. These structures are believed to have been used for religious or sacramental purposes, and also for a sepulcher, as beneath these, imbedded in the earth, were found buried many half-burned human remains, with fragments of pottery and charcoal. These works bear a strong resemblance to temple mounds found elsewhere, but their great extent, encircling so large a tract of land, is evidence that they were intended for a fortification as well as for religious or ceremonial purposes.

ANCIENT FORTIFICATIONS AT MARSEILLES.

On the north side of the Illinois River, about midway of the great rapids, and close to the town of Marseilles, can still be seen an ancient fortification, consisting of low earthworks. These works are located on the river bank fifteen feet above high-water mark, and partly surrounded by a slough or bayou, leaving only a narrow tongue of land between the river and pond, which appears to have been the only ingress and egress to the fort. The fort is of an elongated shape, three hundred yards in length, and will average about thirty yards in breadth, and contains within this enclosure two and three-fourths acres. The walls are irregular, running in and out of a parallel line, with a ditch on the inside. From a military stand-point these works are well located, being situated near the river bank, where the strong current of the rapids is thrown near the shore, and boats could not pass up or down the stream without coming close to the fort.

Northeast of the old fort, on the bluff, about one hundred rods distant, is the remains of earthworks, following the brow of the hill in a straight line, and three hundred feet in length. By some people this is thought to have been an out-post or signal station for the fort on the river, but it is more likely to have been breastworks thrown up by an enemy while besieging the garrison.

Within the old fortification and its surroundings many relics of past ages have been found, but these articles throw no light on the perplexed questions of the time, and by whom these works were constructed. Among these relics is a sword, two silver crosses bearing the letters R C, and with the word "Montreal" stamped on them, also pieces of silver plate for ornamenting gun barrels, knife handles, etc., marked in a like manner, all bearing the initials of the great explorer, Robert Cavalier (La Salle being only a title). In all probability these articles were manufactured at Montreal for La Salle, brought west as part of his stock-in-trade and sold to the Indians, as similar articles marked in like manner have been found elsewhere.

These old earthworks were surveyed by Colonel

D. F. Hitt, of Ottawa, in June, 1876, and a diagram of them can be found in Baldwin's history of La Salle county. Dr. J. H. Goodell, of Marseilles, has made some examination of these relics of antiquity, and to him I am indebted for many of the items given above.

THE RUINED FORT ON FOX RIVER.

This ancient fortification is situated on a bluff on the east side of Fox River, and opposite the mouth of Indian Creek. The bluff on which the fort stands is sixty-five feet high. About forty feet of this is a rock, rising almost perpendicular from the bed of the river, and affords a commanding view of the surroundings. These works are located at the intersection of a deep ravine, and partly surrounded on three sides by a rocky cliff. The land side opposite to the river and ravine is encircled by three rows of breastworks, and on the inside of these is a ditch. Through these rows of breastworks to the eastward is an open gateway, constituting the only egress and ingress to and from the fort within.

On the opposite side of the ravine, on a bluff north of the fort, are a number of mounds. The object for which these were constructed has not been determined. Near these mounds is a chasm cut in the rocky cliff, which is supposed to have been used as a stairway by the occupants of the fort.

The Fox River fort differs from all other ancient works found in this section of the country, as it contains three rows of breastworks, which are close together and extend all the way around it. These old ruins are of a circular form, and contain within the inclosure a little less than one acre of ground.

There are different opinions about the builders of other fortifications in this section of the country, but all agree that the Fox River fort is the work of a prehistoric race, and built centuries ago.

This fort, like the one at Marseilles, was surveyed by Colonel D. F. Hitt, of Ottawa, June 3, 1877, and a diagram of it published in Baldwin's history of La Salle county.

MEDORE JENNETTE, A FUR TRADER.

In 1772 Auguste and Pierre Chouteau, fur traders at St. Louis, extended their business into the Illinois country, and established a trading-post at the mouth of Fox River. Three years before the Illinois Indians were exterminated, and the country occupied by Pottawatomies, whose villages were found at different places along the Illinois River. For many years merchants at Peoria had monopolized the fur trade in this section of the country, but the Chouteaus, who were doing a large business along the upper Mississippi and Missouri rivers, now came in competition with them. Among Chouteau's employes was a young Frenchman named Medore Jennette, who had been raised near St. Vincent, on the Wabash, among Pottawatomie Indians, and spoke their language. Jennette traveled extensively over the country, making the acquaintance of different bands, and enlisted them in favor of his employers' enterprise. After roving a few years he found a home at an Indian village, opposite the mouth of Fox River, where he spent the remainder of his days. Jennette married a squaw, built a cabin in the village. and raised a family of half-breed children. His time was occupied in collecting furs and pelts, shipping them to St. Louis, and the vessel loaded back with goods for the Indian market. It is a fact worthy of note that while Chouteaus and traders at Kaskaskia sent their furs to New Orleans, and from there received their goods, merchants at Peoria continued to trade at Montreal until their town was burned, in 1812.

In the summer of 1773, when Pat Kennedy and comrades ascended the Illinois River in search of copper mines, they employed Jennette to pilot them through the country. These adventurers found coal banks, a saline spring where people were engaged in making salt, and a flint rock where the French obtained their mill-stones, but copper, the object of their search, they found none.

Jennette lived many years among the Indians, became very popular with them, and through his energy and industry his employers accumulated much of their wealth. After his death the family left their Indian home for a French settlement on the Mississippi, where many of his descendants now live. One of his sons, Louis Jennette, although having passed his ninetieth birthday has a vivid recollection of the country along the Illinois River as it appeared eighty years ago. Last summer the old gentleman, accompanied by his grandson, visited the place of his nativity, in order that he might once more look upon the scenes of his childhood. Here, on the south side of the river, is the mineral spring, and here, too, is the spring of sweet water. By the side of it stood his father's cabin, in which he spent his infantile years. North of the river, on the little prairie where he had gathered flowers, and played beneath the shade of outspreading oaks in his boyhood days, is now covered by the city of Ottawa. The river continues to run as in former times; Buffalo Rock, Starved Rock and Maiden's Leap remain the same as in his youthful days, but all the surroundings have undergone a great change. Instead of a wild country of eighty years ago farms are seen in close succession, while towns and cities abound everywhere throughout the land.

CHAPTER XVII.

ENGLISH AND FRENCH RELATION WITH INDIANS.

THE French were liberal in their gifts to the Indians, supplying them with medals and showy trinkets, with which they decorated their persons. They also lived with them in a wigwam, adopting their habits and customs, making of them chums and associates. Many of the French pioneers abandoned their countrymen, sacrificing every tie of blood and kindred, identifying themselves with Indians, and sank into barbarism. In the camp men were found speaking the French language, yet in their barbarous costume, face painted, head decorated with feathers, wearing rings and beads, appearing in every respect like those with whom they had cast their lot, which accords with an old saying, "it is impossible for an Indian to turn paleface, but it is easy for a paleface to turn Indian." Among the English fur traders, hunters and early pioneers were found men low and brutal in their habits, having thrown off all restraint of civilization, making themselves barbarians, but they did not become Indians.

The English, unlike the French, did not court the friendship of the Indians, but would encroach upon their hunting-grounds, treat their rights with contempt, and pay off these injuries in abuse and threats. The difference in these nationalities was soon observed by the Indians, when they formed a strong friendship for one and a dislike for the other, consequently the Indian raids on the settlements were against American citizens only, and no French family was molested. During the different Indian wars in the early settlement of Illinois the French traders and hunters pursued their business unmolested, but if a person was found among them speaking the English language, although employed by the French traders, he would be tomahawked as a common enemy.

AMERICAN PIONEERS OF ILLINOIS.

A number of persons who accompanied Colonel Clark in his expedition against Illinois, being pleased with the country, returned with their families a few years afterward and became the first American pioneers of the territory. Most of these emigrants were from Kentucky, and they made a settlement northeast of Cahokia in what is now St. Clair and Madison counties.

In the summer of 1785 the Kickapoo Indians, headed by their old chief Pecan, commenced hostilities against the American settlers, for the purpose of driving them out of the country. With the exception of a short interval this war continued for ten years, and many of the early settlers were killed or carried off captive by these savages. Among the emigrants from Kentucky were three families of Whitesides, who became noted Indian fighters, and the history of these wars is filled with many of their heroic acts and wild adventures.

The emigrants who located in or near the French villages were not molested, as the war was carried on against the Americans only. During the continuation of this war no French family was molested, and the traders continued to pass up and down the Illinois River in the pursuit of their business the same as in time of peace.

In 1786 the Indians made prisoners of two small children belonging to Samuel Garrison, carried them to their village on the Saline fork of Sangamon River, where they were kept for about a year, but were finally ransomed by Colonel N. Jarret, of Cahokia.

EARLY GOVERNMENT OF ILLINOIS.

From the early settlement of Illinois there was no law in force but village ordinances till 1711, when a patent was granted to Crozat, a Paris merchant, for the purpose of governing the country. Captain

La Mott, an agent of Crozat, came to Illinois, acting as governor, and extended civil jurisdiction over the different colonies. Five years afterward a new patent was granted to the Louisiana Mining Company, with George Law, a Scotch banker, as its head, and for fourteen years this company governed the country. The charter of this company having expired in 1732, the country reverted back to the crown, and Colonel D. Artaguette appointed governor. In 1765 the British took possession of Illinois, by virtue of a treaty between France and England made some time before. For a short time Captain Stirling acted as governor, and was succeeded by different commanders, who enforced laws contrary to the wishes of the French people. In 1778 Colonel Clark took possession of Illinois, and it became a part of the State of Virginia. The same year the territory was organized by extending over it civil jurisdiction, and known as Illinois county, Virginia. Colonel John Todd, of Kentucky, received an appointment from the Governor of Virginia, as Lieutenant-Commandant, with power to enforce laws, and governed the country for three years, but while on a visit to Kentucky in 1782 was killed at the battle of Blue Licks.

Virginia having relinquished her claim to Illinois in 1784, an ordinance passed Congress transferring it to the general government, consequently it became a part of the Northwest Territory, and was divided into two counties, Randolph and St. Clair. In 1809 it was set off into a separate territory, and Ninian Edwards, of Kentucky, appointed governor. In 1812 it assumed a second grade of territorial government, with a legislature and a delegate in Congress. In 1818 Illinois became a state, and Shadrack Bond elected the first governor.

DISAPPEARANCE OF BUFFALO.

The flesh of the buffalo furnished the Indians with food, their skins with clothing, bedding, tents, etc., their sinews for bows, the bones for ornaments, and the hair they wove into a fine fabric for dress, consequently the disappearance of these animals from the country deprived them of many luxuries. The exact time the buffalo left the country has been a controverted point, but in comparing various accounts it must have been between the years of 1780 and 1790. In 1778 Antonie Des Champs, a noted Indian trader, came to Peoria with his parents, and continued to live there until the town was burned. He says for many years after he came west buffalo were plenty throughout the country, and large herds of them were frequently seen swimming the Illinois River.

I have conversed with old Indians that were born and raised in this part of the country, who said in their youthful days they had seen large herds of buffalo on these prairies, but they all perished at the time of a big snow which covered the ground many feet in depth, and crusted so hard on top that people walked on it. Next spring a few buffalo, poor and haggard in appearance, were seen going westward, and as they approached the carcasses of dead ones, which were lying in great numbers here and there on the prairie, they would stop, commence pawing and lowing, then start off again in a lope westward, and from that time they were seldom seen east of the Mississippi River.

Forty years ago buffalo bones were plenty on these prairies and in many places acres of ground were covered with them, showing where large herds had perished. Skulls with horns still on them were frequently found, and their trails leading to and from watering-places were plain to be seen in the early settlement of the country.

EARLY HISTORY OF CHICAGO.

All that is known of the early history of Chicago, or the place where the city now stands, is taken from Indian tradition and scraps of the early explorer's journal, neither of which is considered very reliable.

It is said Father Nicollet, a French Jesuit priest, preached to the Indians at the mouth of Chicago River in 1640, and in all probability he was the first white man that ever rowed a canoe on the waters of Lake Michigan, or trod the soil of Illinois. In 1671 Nicholas Barret visited this place, and two years afterward Marquette and comrades stopped here. According to tradition a Frenchman named Goris built a trading-house on Chicago River and surrounded it with palisades, called a fort, but the time of building it is not known. In the early settlement of Chicago relics of a fortification were found on the north branch, a short distance above the forks of the river. In General Wayne's treaty at Greenville, in 1796 a purchase was made of the Indians, six miles square, at the mouth of Chicago River, where a fort once stood, is the language of the treaty. About the year 1796 a negro named Jean Baptiste built a cabin at the mouth of Chicago River and occupied it for a short time. This cabin was occupied for some years by a French fur trader by the name of Le Mai, who sold it to John Kinzie in 1804.

In the fall of 1803 Captain John Whitler, with a company of soldiers, came from Detroit in a schooner and built Fort Dearborn. The next year John Kinzie, a fur trader, came to Chicago, and occupied Baptiste's cabin on the north side of the river, opposite the fort. Antiona Oulmette, Charles Lee and Mr. Claybourn came here soon after the fort was built. Kinzie, Oulmette and Claybourn were engaged in the fur trade, but Lee was a farmer, and made a large farm at a grove of timber on the south branch called "Lee's Place," afterward Bridgeport.

JEAN BAPTISTE AND FATHER BONNER

There lived near Lexington, Kentucky, a slave named Jean Baptiste, who had been a captive among the Indians, learned their language, and became fascinated with their free and easy manner of living About the year 1790 Baptiste became dissatisfied with restraint; his proud spirit could not be subdued by the whip of the master, therefore he severed the bonds which made him a slave. Armed with his master's rifle, a large hunting-knife, and taking the north star for a guide, he became a free man. After traveling a long way through a wild country he came to an Indian village on the Des Plaines River, where he found refuge, and became an Indian in life and habit. Here he married a squaw and raised a family of children. One of his grandsons is now living in a hewed-log house on the bank of Cahokia Creek, in St. Clair county, and from whom I obtained the narrative relating to his distinguished grandsire.

The Indians used to say the first white man that lived in Chicago was a negro. This negro was Jean Baptiste, whose name is associated with the early history of the great metropolis of the west. He left the Indian village on the Des Plaines soon after coming to the country, and built a cabin near the lake on the north side of Chicago River. He cultivated a small piece of ground, spent much of his time in hunting and fishing, and concocted schemes to make himself a chief among the Indians. He told the Indians that he had been a great chief among the whites, and expected to become one among them. He tried to induce his Indian friends to move their village to the mouth of Chicago River, telling them it would be a big town some day, and they could sell the land to white people at a good price. His object was to have a village here on the lake shore, of which he would be the founder, and by that means become a chief. A few lodges were built here, in accordance with Baptiste's wishes, but the scattering trees afforded them but little protection from the cold winds off the lake, so they left and returned to their old village on the Des Plaines.

At that time Father Bonner, a missionary, was living among the Indians, and for many years had preached to them. Baptiste, aware of the priest's influence among the Indians, thought he might use it to his own advantage, therefore he sought his friendship and gained his confidence. He also joined the church, became a zealous Catholic, attended all meetings, and made long and fervent prayers. Father Bonner thought only of making Baptiste an instrument in his hands to promote the cause of Christianity, while the unscrupulous negro expected to use the priest in advancing his claims to the chieftainship, therefore the two became intimate friends and labored for each other's interest.

On St. Jerome's day a big meeting was held among the Indian converts, and after preaching Father Bonner told his hearers that it had been impressed on his mind that Baptiste should be a ruler among them, and went through the process of anointing him chief. The Indians refused to accept Baptiste as their chief, notwithstanding he had been appointed by high authority. Failing to be made a chief Baptiste became disgusted with the life of a savage, abandoned his cabin, and went to Peoria, where he ended his days.

CHAPTER XVIII.

EARLY FRENCH SETTLEMENT AT PEORIA.

AT what time the French commenced a settlement at Peoria has long been a controverted point, on which both history and tradition are alike defective. Some people believe it commenced in 1680, when La Salle built Fort Crève-Cœur, and from that time people continued to reside here. Others date the permanent settlement in 1760, but from old letters and manuscripts now in the possession of the descendants of early pioneers it is evident that it commenced at an early period. I have given this subject much attention, by comparing scraps of history, extracts of letters from Jesuit priests, and conversing with the descendants of the early settlers, some of whom trace their genealogy back to the time of La Salle. By comparing all the different accounts relating thereto, I think it is shown conclusively that the settlement at Peoria commenced in the year 1711, and under the following circumstances:

In the summer of 1711 Father Marest, a Jesuit priest from Canada, preached to the Indians at Cahokia, and by the force of his eloquence many were converted to Christianity. Among these converts was a chief named Kolet, from Peoria Lake, who at that time was visiting friends at Cahokia. This chief prevailed on Father Marest to accompany him home to his village and proclaim salvation to his people. Late in November the priest and chief, accompanied by two warriors, left for Peoria in a bark canoe, but after a journey of ten leagues the river froze up, so that further progress by water was out of the question. The travelers hid their canoe, with most of their baggage, in the thick timber at the mouth of a creek, and continued their journey on foot. For twelve days they waded through snow and water, crossing big prairies, and through thick timber full of briers and thorns. At night they slept on dry grass or leaves gathered from under the snow, without shelter or anything but their blankets to protect them from the cold winter blasts. The provision for their journey as well as their bedding was left with the canoe, consequently they were obliged to subsist on wild grapes, and game killed by the way. After many days of fatigue and exposure, their limbs frost-bitten, and their bodies reduced in flesh by starvation, they at last reached the village, and from its inhabitants received a hearty welcome.

This Indian village (afterward called by the

French Opa) was situated on the west bank of Peoria Lake, one and a half miles above its outlet. On LaSalle's first visit to this place, thirty-one years before, he found here a large town, and was cordially received by the head chief, Niconape, but this chief had long since been gathered to his fathers, and his place occupied by Kolet, above referred to.

Father Marest found quarters in an Indian lodge, and remained here at the village until spring without meeting with any of his countrymen. He preached to the Indians almost daily, many of whom embraced Christianity, and their names were afterward enrolled in the church book.

In the following spring, 1712, the French at Fort St. Louis established a trading-post here at Peoria Lake, and a number of families came thither from Canada and built cabins in the Indian village. For fifty years French and half-breeds continued to live in the town with the Indians as one people, and during that time peace and harmony prevailed between them. It is true Charlevoix while visiting this country in 1721 says he found no one living at Fort Crève-Cœur, which was five miles below this village, but met with his countrymen at different places along the Illinois River.

In 1723 the Royal Louisiana Company granted to Philip Renault a tract of land fifteen leagues square, near the village of Peoria. This grant was bounded as follows: Commencing at the town of Peoria, running down the river fifteen leagues, west fifteen leagues, thence north fifteen leagues, and east to the place of beginning. This land grant, equal to three counties, was considered of no value at the time, and the claim was not enforced by the heirs of Renault, like the other two grants near Fort Chartres, consequently it reverted back to the crown.

Here at the village of Peoria Father Senat built a chapel, and made many converts among his red brethren. The time this chapel was built is unknown, but must have been previous to 1736, for in that year he was burned at the stake by the Chickasaw Indians in lower Louisiana.

In the course of time the village of Peoria was abandoned for one which figured in after years more extensively, and known in history as La Ville de Maillet.

LA VILLE DE MAILLET.

In the spring of 1761 Robert Maillet, a trader at Peoria, built a dwelling one and a half miles below the town, near the outlet of the lake, and moved his family thither. Here the land raised gradually from the water's edge until it reached the high prairie in the rear, forming a beautiful sloping plateau, probably unequaled by any place on the Illinois River.

This location for a town was considered preferable to the old one, the land dryer, the water better, and thought to be more healthy, consequently others built houses by the side of Maillet's, and it soon became quite a village. A short time afterward the inhabitants deserted the old town for the new, and no Frenchman remained in the old village after 1770, but it was occupied by Indians for many years. The houses vacated by the French were occupied by Indians until they rotted down, and the remains of an old chapel could be seen here long after the dwellings had disappeared.

This new town took the name of La Ville de Maillet (that is, the city of Maillet) after its founder, and it was in existence fifty-one years. A fort was built here consisting of two block houses surrounded by earthworks and palisades, with an open gateway to the south, next to the town, and was only intended as a place of retreat in case of trouble with the Indians. This fort was never occupied, except a short time by Robert Maillet, who used one of the block houses for a dwelling and the other for the sale of goods. Some years afterward Maillet left the fort for a more desirable place of residence and trade, and it remained vacant for many years; the inclosure within the stockades being used by the citizens in common for a cow-yard.

In 1820 Hypolite Maillet, in his sworn testimony before Edward Cole, register of the land-office at Edwardsville, in relation to French claims, said that he was forty-five years old, and born in a stockade fort which stood near the southern extremity of Peoria Lake. In the winter of 1788 a party of Indians came to Peoria to trade, and, in accordance with their former practice, took quarters in the fort, but getting on a drunken spree they burned it down. In the spring of 1819, when Americans commenced a settlement here at Peoria, the outlines of the old French fort were plain to be seen on the high ground near the lake, and a short distance above the present site of the Chicago and Rock Island depot. The line of earthworks could be traced out by the small embankments, and in some places pieces of pickets were found above ground. Back of the fort was the remains of a blacksmith shop, and near it grew up a wild plum tree. This plum tree was dug up by John Brisket, the owner of the land, and under it was found a vault containing a quantity of old metal, among which were a number of gun barrels, knives, tomahawks, copper and brass trinkets, etc. Among other things found in the vault were pieces of silver and brass plate for inlaying gun stocks and ornamenting knife handles. These things appeared to have been the stock-in-trade of a gun-smith, and, for some cause unknown, buried here.*

According to the statements of Antoine Des Champs, Thomas Forsyth, and others, who had long been residents of Peoria previous to its destruction in 1812, we infer that the town contained a large population. It formed a connecting link between the settlements on the Mississippi and Canada, and being situated in the midst of an Indian country, caused it to be a fine place for the fur trade. The town was built along the beach of the lake, and to each house was attached an outlet for a garden, which extended back on the prairie. The houses were all constructed of wood, one story high, with porches on two sides, and located in a garden surrounded with fruit and flowers. Some of the dwellings were built of hewed timbers set upright, and the space between the posts filled in with stone and mortar, while others were built of hewed logs notched together after the style of a pioneer's cabin. The floors were laid with puncheons, and the chimney built with mud and sticks.

When Colonel Clark took possession of Illinois in 1778 he sent three soldiers, accompanied by two Frenchmen, in a canoe to Peoria to notify the people that they were no longer under British rule but citizens of the United States. Among these soldiers

* Ballance's history of Peoria.

was a man named Nicholas Smith, a resident of Bourbon county, Kentucky, and whose son, Joseph Smith (Dod Joe), was among the first American settlers of Peoria. Through this channel we have an account of Peoria as it appeared a century ago, and it agrees well with other traditional accounts.

Mr. Smith said Peoria at the time of his visit was a large town, built along the beach of the lake, with narrow, unpaved streets, and houses constructed of wood. Back of the town were gardens, stock-yards, barns, etc., and among these was a wine-press, with a large cellar or under-ground vault for storing wine. There was a church with a large wooden cross raised above the roof, and with gilt lettering over the door. There was an unoccupied fort on the bank of the lake, and close by it a wind-mill for grinding grain. The town contained six stores or places of trade, all of which were well filled with goods for the Indian market. The inhabitants consisted of French, half-breeds and Indians, not one of whom could understand or speak English.

FRENCH INHABITANTS OF PEORIA.

The inhabitants of Peoria consisted principally of French emigrants from Canada, many of whom were traders, hunters, voyageurs or boatmen. From that happy faculty of adapting themselves to their situation for which the French people are so remarkable they lived in harmony with their savage neighbors for three succeeding generations. Being far away from all other civilized communities they made friends and associates of the natives, and intermarried with them, consequently their prosperity at the present time shows strong marks of Indian lineage. The traders were men of education and energy, but the masses being illiterate, possessed but little property, and less enterprise, enjoying the present without regard to the future. They were a contented, happy people, never troubling themselves with the affairs of government, nor indulging in political strifes, but cheerfully obeying the priests and king's officer. They lived in a fruitful country, which abounded in game, where the necessaries of life could be obtained with but little labor, and having no tax or tribute to pay to the government they became indolent and spent much of their time in idleness.

Those engaged in merchandising turned their attention almost exclusively to the traffic with the Indians, adapting themselves to their customs and habits, and many of them seeking alliance in marriage. The boatmen were active and sprightly. With all the vivacity of the French character they had but little of the intemperance and brutal coarseness usually found among boatmen and marines. Their boats were small, many of them bark canoes, and with skill these light crafts were run up swift currents, while the toil of the oarsmen was enlivened with songs and demonstrations of mirth. As hunters they roamed over the wide plains of the west to the Rocky Mountains, sharing the hospitality of the natives, abiding with them for a long time, and in some cases permanently.

The French citizens of Peoria were a quiet, peaceable people, ignorant and superstitious, and much influenced by the priests. Having no public schools but few of them except the priests and merchants could read or write, but in manners, conversation and refinement they compared well with educated people. Out of eighteen claimants for the land where the city of Peoria now stands all but three signed their names with a mark, and it is said not a woman among them could read or write.

Among the inhabitants of Peoria were merchants or traders who made annual trips to Canada in canoes, carrying thither pelts and furs, and loaded back with goods for the Indian market. They were blacksmiths, wagon-makers, carpenters, shoemakers, etc., and most of the implements used in farming were of home manufacture. Although isolated from the civilized world, and surrounded by savages, their standard of morality was high; theft, robbery or murder were seldom heard of. They were a gay, happy people, having many social parties, wine suppers, balls and public festivals. They lived in harmony with the Indians, who were their neighbors and friends, adopting in part their customs, and in trade with them accumulated most of their wealth.

FRENCH COSTUMES AND MANNERS.

The dress of both men and women was very plain, made of coarse material, and the style of their wardrobe was partly European and partly Indian. The men seldom wore a hat, cap or coat, their heads being covered with a cotton handkerchief, folded on the crown like a night-cap or an Arabian turban. Instead of a coat they wore a loose blanket garment called capote, with a cap of the same material hanging down at the back of the neck, which could be drawn over the head as a protection from rain or cold. The women wore loose dresses, made mostly of coarse material, their heads covered with a hood or blanket, and their long hair hanging down their back like an Indian squaw. But these women were noted for sprightliness in conversation, with grace and elegance of manners, and notwithstanding the plainness of their dress many of them were not lacking in personal charms.

Although long since separated from civilized society they retain much of the refinement and politeness so common to their race; and it is a remarkable fact that the roughest hunter or boatsman among them could appear in a ball-room or at a gay party with the ease and grace of a well-bred gentleman.

The French people at Peoria being isolated from civilization were free from many of its vices, and appeared to be perfectly contented with their manner of living. According to the statements of their numerous descendants they lived a life of alternate toil and pleasure, with much gayety and innocent amusements, and were a contented, happy people.

FRENCH LAND CLAIMS.

The French settled at Peoria without a grant or permission from any government, and the title to the land was derived from possession only. But these titles were valid according to usage, as well as by a village ordinance, and lands were bought and sold the same as if patented by government. Each person had a right to claim any portion of the unoccupied land, and when in possession his title was regarded perfect, and could be bought and sold the same as other real estate. Each citizen had a village lot for a garden attached to his residence, and if a farmer a portion of the common field. On the prairie west of the town were extensive farms all enclosed in one field, each person contributing his share of fencing, and the time of securing the crop and pasturing the stocks was regulated by a town ordinance. The boundaries of these farms could be traced out in the early settlement at Peoria, and a large tract of land lying between the river and bluff showed marks of having been cultivated.

When the French settlement commenced at Peoria the country belonged to France, afterward to Great Britain, and lastly to the United States, but these changes did not effect the people in any way. When Illinois came under the British rule, in 1765, Captain Stirling, commanding, at Fort Chartres, sent messengers to Peoria to notify the people that they were British subjects. In 1778, when Illinois came under United States authority, they were again notified of the change in the government, but they still remained French in feeling and sympathy. They claimed no allegiance to any government, acknowledged no law except their own village ordinance, and paid no tax to any power. While these people were living in peace and harmony (as they believed), with all the world, being separated nearly two hundred miles from civilization, they were attacked by an armed force, their dwellings burned, and all the heads of families carried off prisoners of war, as will be narrated in the succeeding chapter.

In 1820 eighteen persons, heads of families, filed papers in Edwardsville laud office, claiming the land on which the city of Peoria now stands. The depositions were taken by the register, Edward Coles, afterward Governor of Illinois, and all the testimony relating to their claims is now on file among the state papers. Coles was a man of an inquiring turn of mind, fond of antique history, and made a full report of the testimony to the land department. For many years the claimants prosecuted their case in the different courts, and at last succeeded in getting a large amount of money from the occupants of the land.

CHAPTER XIX.

PIERRE DE BEURO, AN INDIAN TRADER.

IN the year 1776 a young Frenchman named Pierre de Beuro, of Cahokia, came to Peoria, and for a time clerked in a trading-house. Being of an enterprising turn of mind, and understanding the Indian language, he concluded to visit chiefs whose acquaintance he formed while at Peoria. While on these visits he married a daughter of a noted chief, who had a village near the mouth of Fox River, and concluded to establish a trading-post in the midst of the Indian country. After getting a promise of patronage of all the neighboring villages he went to Cahokia, to make the necessary arrangements to go into business.

Below the mouth of Bureau Creek is an elevated piece of land, covered with timber, and known as Hickory Ridge. This place became a noted landmark among the French and Indians, and has been the scene of a number of traditionary incidents. It also became a place of note in the early settlement of the country, and during high water a landing for the Hennepin ferry-boat. Here on this ridge, elevated above the floods of the river, De Beuro built a double log-cabin, and laid the foundation of a large fur trade. Being patronized by all the surrounding village he had a large trade, sending his furs to Cahokia and receiving goods in return. Antoine des Champs said that every spring for a number of years canoes loaded with furs and buffalo robes passed Peoria from this trading-house. The traders at Peoria became unfriendly toward De Beuro, as he injured their business, and offered to buy him out, but he refused to sell to them.

In the spring of 1790 De Beuro, according to custom, sent three canoes loaded with furs to Cahokia, in charge of his clerk and two Indians. The trader accompanied the canoes down the river about twenty miles to an Indian village, and from here left for home on foot, but never reached it. Search being made for the missing trader, his remains were found some days afterward, where he had been murdered and partly devoured by wolves. Report says a trader at Peoria, whose descendants are now living near East St. Louis, employed a half-breed to assassinate De Beuro, and thereby break up the rival trading-post. A large number of warriors went to Peoria and demanded the supposed murderer, threatening to burn the town if not given up, but on being convinced that the murderer had fled they left for their homes.

When the clerk learned that De Beuro was dead he appropriated the proceeds of the furs to his own account, and his wife put the goods in canoes and took them to her father's village.*

TECUMSEH AT PEORIA.

Tecumseh after meeting General Harrison in council at Vincennes, in August, 1810, came west for the purpose of enlisting the different tribes in a war against the frontier settlements. He made an extensive tour in the western country, going as far north as Green Bay, and south through Missouri and Arkansas, and in the following year traveled among the Creeks and Chickasaws in the southern states. While traveling through the country he visited Peoria, and was the guest of Francis Racine, an old acquaintance of his, who had traded with his band on the Wabash for many years. Tecumseh was accompanied by three chiefs, all dressed in white buckskin, with eagle feathers in their head-dress, and mounted on spirited black ponies. The visitors made a short stay at Peoria. On learning that the

* A few years ago David Miller cut the timber off Hickory Ridge, and put the land under cultivation. Where De Beuro's trading-house stood many relics of civilization, such as pieces of dishes, glass-ware, etc., were plowed up in cultivating the ground.

French disapproved of their plans, and not wishing to offend them, they left without having a talk with the Indians who were encamped near the town. At Gomo's village the travelers were met by a large number of warriors, many of whom had come from neighboring villages to listen to Tecumseh's stirring eloquence in behalf of his great scheme of uniting all the tribes of the west and driving the palefaces out of the country.

Gomo, Black Partridge, Senachwine and Comas were visited by Tecumseh and his friends, but they all refused to accede to his plans, preferring to remain at peace.

INDIAN DEPREDATIONS.

In the summer of 1810 a party of Indians belonging on the Illinois River stole a number of horses from the settlers, who pursued the thieves for two days. At night while the settlers were asleep around a camp-fire the Indians returned and fired on them, killing three and wounding two others. The authorities made a demand on the Indians for these murderers, but no attention was paid to it. In the following summer Governor Edwards sent Captain Samuel Levering, with a company of men, in a keel-boat to Peoria with instructions to make a formal demand of the Indians for a surrender of these murderers. Captain Levering and his comrades were French (some of them half-breeds), understanding the Indian language, and between whom a friendly relation existed, even in the time of war. On arriving at Peoria the visitors were cordially received by both French and Indians, who prepared a feast for them, with a ball in the evening. Some of the guests were fascinated with Indian maidens, two of whom took wives home with them.

Joseph Trotier, of Cahokia, accompanied by two half-breeds, ascended the river in a canoe to the great bend, stopping at all the Indian villages on their route, and from the chiefs and warriors received many pledges of peace and friendship. This party visited the village of Wappa, on Bureau Creek, and the head chief, Comas, sent as a present to Governor Edwards a large pair of elk horns, also a pair of dressed bear and panther skins, all of which were taken with his own hands. Trotier made arrangements with the chiefs and principal warriors to meet in council at Peoria on the following week and hear the message sent them by the governor read.

At the time appointed the Indians came to Peoria, heard the governor's message read, and a speech made to them by Captain Levering. The message and speech was replied to by talks from a number of chiefs, in which they pledged themselves to use all proper means to capture the murderers and deliver them up to the authorities for punishment. Captain Levering after performing his mission, with his comrades, returned to the settlement, carrying thither many presents from the chiefs to Governor Edwards, together with their pledges of friendship and good will.

Captain Levering while at Peoria delivered a commission, signed by the governor, to Thomas Forsyth as justice of the peace, also one to John Baptiste Dufond as captain of militia. These commissions bear date August 8, 1811, and both of these papers are now in the hands of descendants of the parties.

General William Clark, of St. Louis, was general Indian agent for the western country, but Governor Edwards acted also as sub-agent within the territory of Illinois.

INDIAN COUNCIL AT CAHOKIA.

During the winter of 1811 and 1812 the Indians on the Illinois River heard through a half-breed who came from the settlement that preparations were being made to send an army against them in the spring unless the murderers were given up. On learning of these facts they became very much alarmed, and some of the chiefs went to Peoria to consult with their friends, and procure their assistance in averting the evil which threatened them. In their behalf Captain Maillet consented to go and see the governor, and inform him that the murderers had fled from the country and could not be delivered up, but the Indians proposed to furnish a like number of young braves to be executed in their stead.

On arriving at Kaskaskia Captain Maillet laid the case before the governor, who authorized him to assure the chiefs that the matter of peace or war depended entirely upon their own acts.

In the following March Governor Edwards sent Captain Hebert on a mission among these Indians, requesting them to meet him in council at Cahokia. Captain Hebert was also instructed to notify all the traders at Peoria to close their stores,—giving up all trade with the Indians until this trouble was settled. The traders were informed unless they complied with the governor's demands they need not expect any indulgence from the government in case of war, but they paid no attention to this order.

Captain Hebert collected many of the principal chiefs and brought them with him to Cahokia, where the governor by agreement met them in council. This council was held on the 16th of April, 1812, in a little grove of timber on the bank of Cahokia Creek, above the town, and attended by a large number of citizens.* Speeches were made by different chiefs in reply to the governor's address, and with new pledges of friendship the Indians were dismissed with many presents. After this council for a time confidence between the white and red man appeared to have been restored, but this was of short duration. An evil-disposed person circulated false reports about the Indians making preparations for war, and the settlers were very much alarmed.

In reading the many letters written by Governor Edwards to the secretary of war a person would believe that war with the Indians was inevitable, but the facts in the case do not warrant this conclusion. During the summer of 1812 forts were built, militia kept under arms, and the general government called on for troops to defend the territory. Rumors were circulated that a large body of Indian warriors were collected near Peoria, armed, and painted for war, and it was believed that they intended to descend the river in canoes to make a raid on the settlement.

* While on a recent visit to Cahokia the place where this council assembled was pointed out to me by an old man who attended it. Although a boy of only twelve years of age at that time he recollects the appearance of some of the chiefs, and, understanding the Indian language, can repeat parts of their speeches. Gomo, Senachwine and Black Partridge were the principal orators, and their eloquence and commanding appearance made a lasting impression upon his then youthful mind.

In this grove where the council was held is an old burr-oak tree by the creek bank which marks the spot where a number of incidents occurred in early times. At the root of this tree, tradition says, Pontiac (or the Indian who passed for such) was sitting when a drunken Indian came up behind him and split his head open with his tomahawk.

To prevent a surprise from these savages Captain Whitesides, with a company of volunteers, in a heavy planked gunboat, lay for three months above the mouth of the Illinois River to prevent the Indians from descending it to attack the settlements. While these preparations for war were continued by the authorities of the territory the Indians were quietly pursuing their hunting, making no provision for either an attack or defense, and when troops marched against them they were taken by surprise.

From what is now known of these affairs it appears evident that Governor Edwards was imposed upon by unscrupulous men, who made false reports with regard to the Indians. The governor employed a man named John Hays to examine into Indian affairs to ascertain the number of bands, the name and location of villages, with their inhabitants, etc. These reports made by Hays were false in almost every particular, and, to make the matter worse, the governor copied these reports in his letters to the secretary of war, and therefore became a part of the state papers. While Governor Edwards was a man of ability, and made a good executive officer, so far as relates to his duties as governor of the territory, yet as an Indian agent he proved himself a failure, having become the dupe of designing men. I have talked with many of the French residents of Peoria and their descendants, also with Indians who were born and raised in villages along the Illinois River, and know whereof I write.

ILLINOIS TERRITORY AT THE TIME OF THE BRITISH WAR.

At the commencement of the late British war there was within the limits of the Illinois territory less than twelve thousand people, a large portion of whom were native French citizens and emigrants from Kentucky. The settlement extended along the Mississippi River for about sixty miles, from the mouth of Kaskaskia River to a station opposite Columbia, eight miles below Alton. There was a settlement on the Ohio River at Shawneetown, also one at Saline, or United States Salt Works, protected by a rude fortification and a few soldiers. The extreme south part of this state was an unbroken wilderness, a hunting-ground for Indians, while the central and northern portion belonged to the natives. With the exception of the country along the Illinois River, and shores of Lake Michigan, the prairies of this state had never been explored by white people to any great extent.

There were but two counties organized, Randolph and St. Clair, and all the country in the northern portion of the state, including Wisconsin, was under the jurisdiction of the latter. Summonses and writs were issued from the circuit court at Cahokia, the seat of justice for St. Clair county, against persons at Prairie du Chien, and in one case property was sold there under an execution issued from that court. The citizens of Peoria, however, would not admit that they were under the jurisdiction of St. Clair county, claiming to be free and independent of all foreign power, and the sheriff could not enforce demands against them.

A FALSE REPORT CIRCULATED.

In the summer of 1812 a vagabond named Elijah Bruce, having committed a lawless act, was driven from Peoria, and found a refuge at Kaskaskia. Bruce had been a resident of Peoria for a number of years, acquainted with all its principal citizens, and, to retaliate on his enemies for driving him away, circulated an evil report about them. He said the French at Peoria were assisting the Indians to make war on the settlements, that two military men were engaged in teaching them war tactics, and preparing them to take the field. He also said the British in Canada had furnished the traders with rifles, powder, tomahawks, knives etc., which were distributed among the Indians free of charge; that Captain J. B. Maillet had stolen cattle from Wood River settlement to feed warriors who were collected at Gomo's village. He further said the day before he left Peoria Francis Racine, a trader, came through from the Sac village on the Mississippi with five packhorses loaded with lead to supply the warriors.

Bruce was an Irishman by birth, a man of education and general intelligence, a good talker, and his story was believed by people generally. But it was afterward proven that these stories were false in every particular, and without any foundation in fact so far as assisting the Indians in making war on the settlement is concerned. It is true the traders at Peoria for many years had been in the habit of bringing from Canada various kinds of goods, including arms, to supply the Indian market, and also packed lead on horses from the Sac village, but this was done in accordance with their legitimate trade. The story about Captain Maillet stealing cattle originated from the fact of his bringing a stray drove back to Peoria that had wandered away down south. The cattle being crossed with buffalo were inclined to ramble, and during the hard winter a herd belonging to the people of Peoria strayed off southward. In the spring these cattle were found on Mackinaw River by Captain Maillet, and driven back to Peoria, as previously stated. Instead of Captain Maillet being a cattle thief, as alleged by the vagabond Bruce, at the close of the war he was rewarded by an act of Congress for his loyalty to the government.

The evil reports circulated by Bruce are said to have been confirmed by another person from Peoria, and by this means a great panic was created among the frontier settlers. Some of them fled from the country, while others abandoned farm labor, and began building forts to protect themselves from threatened hostilities. Governor Edwards believed these rumors, as may be inferred by his letter to the secretary of war, dated August 4, 1812, in which he says: "No troops have arrived in the territory yet, and I think you may count on hearing of a bloody strike on us soon. I have been extremely reluctant to send my family away, but unless assistance comes soon I shall bury my papers in the ground, send off my family, and stand my ground as long as possible."

The inhabitants of Peoria claimed to be foreigners, owing no allegiance to the government, but by a treaty between France and this country, made some years before, all French residents of Illinois became citizens of the United States, and to assist the Indians in making war on the settlers was treason. Governor Edwards, believing the common reports, issued a proclamation calling for volunteers to march against the Indians along the Illinois River, and their allies, the treacherous French at Peoria.

CHAPTER XX.

BLACK PARTRIDGE, A NOTED INDIAN CHIEF.

THIS noted chief, whose Indian name was Muck-oteypokee, had a village at the foot of the bluff on the south side of the Illinois River opposite the head of Peoria Lake. Here he lived and here he died, and in the early settlement of that section of the country his grave was pointed out to strangers. Persons are now living who knew this chief very well, and from whom I obtained a description of his person, and many incidents relating to his life and character.

Black Partridge was tall and slim, with a high forehead, a large nose, a sharp visage, and piercing black eyes. His appearance was fine, his form erect, and his figure commanding, so a stranger could see at a glance that he was no ordinary Indian. The long, coarse hair, once as black as a raven, but of later years mixed with gray, hung in matted clusters around his shoulders. On his breast he wore a silver medal on which was stamped a medallion head of General Washington, and in his nose and ears wore large gold rings.

In the border wars of the west Black Partridge took a part, and with his braves fought against the whites. In 1795 he attended and signed the treaty at Greenville, and received from the hand of General Wayne the medal referred to. This medal as an insignia of peace and friendship was carried about his person for seventeen years, and he surrendered it to Captain Heald, commander of Fort Dearborn, on the evening of August 14, 1812, the day before the troops were massacred, as will be hereafter narrated.

INDIANS RECEIVING THE FIRST TIDINGS OF WAR.

In the summer of 1812 emissaries from the Wabash, said to have been sent by Tecumseh, visited the villages along the Illinois River, bringing with them the startling intelligence that war had been declared between England and the United States. These emissaries explained to the chiefs and warriors who had met in council at Gomo's village that the British offered a large amount of gold to each warrior that joined their standard. They also pointed out to them the great importance of capturing Fort Dearborn before the troops garrisoned there obtained intelligence of the declaration of war. The war-whoop was raised by many of the young braves belonging to different villages, and on the next day they left for Chicago with the intention of attacking the fort. Black Partridge having failed in preventing these young bloods from going to Chicago mounted his pony and followed them.

On arriving at Chicago Black Partridge went to see his old friend John Kinzie, and after a cordial greeting he said to him, "My heart is sad; evil muses have been singing in my ears all day long,— telling me the friendship which for many years has existed between us is about to be severed." For a number of years the old chief had been acquainted with John Kinzie and his family, having been a frequent guest at his house, ate at his table, and trotted the little ones on his knee. Believing that his friends were about to be slain filled his heart with sadness, and while expressing his fears he could not restrain his emotions, but frequently gave way to floods of tears.

On the day before the evacuation of Fort Dearborn the chiefs and principal warriors met in council, and at this council it was decided to massacre the troops on leaving the fort. In this council the voice of Black Partridge was heard for peace, but the war policy prevailed, and with a sorrowful heart this true friend of the whites returned to his camp, knowing that the morrow would be a day of blood and carnage.

On the evening before the Chicago massacre Black Partridge entered the quarters of Captain Heald, the commanding officer of Fort Dearborn, and, after a friendly greeting, said to him, "I have come here to deliver up to you this medal which was given to me by General Wayne as a token of friendship. For many years I have worn this medal on my breast, and it is with a sorrowful heart I now part with it, but our young braves are resolved on imbruing their hands in human blood. I cannot restrain them, and I will not wear an emblem of friendship while I am compelled to act as an enemy."

MRS. HELM'S LIFE SAVED BY BLACK PARTRIDGE.

In Mrs. Kinzie's account of the Chicago massacre an incident is related of Black Partridge saving the life of Mrs. Helm, wife of Lieutenant Helm, and stepdaughter of John Kinzie. This story equals, if not surpasses, the most extravagant flights of romance, but its truth is confirmed by a person now living, Mrs. Besson, who was present at the time, and from whom I obtained in part the following narrative:

On the morning of the 15th of August, 1812, the sun rose with unusual splendor, and its golden rays reflected from the smooth waters of Lake Michigan, but many of the inmates of Fort Dearborn who looked upon this enchanting scenery did not live to see it set beneath the western horizon. At nine o'clock in the morning the troops left the fort, marching in military array, with martial music, and flags waving in the morning breeze. Captain Wells, having his face blackened after the manner of the Indians, with his Miami warriors mounted on ponies, led the van. The troops on foot followed, and next to them were the baggage wagons, containing the sick, with women and children, while the Pottawatomies, five hundred in number, followed in the rear. This caravan took the road along the beach of the lake, for about a mile and a half, to a range of sand knolls.* Here the Indians left the road and took to the prairie, when Captain Wells, with his horse on a gallop, came back and told the troops to form for battle, as they were about to be attacked. Soon the battle commenced, the soldiers defending themselves bravely, selling their lives as dearly as possible, but many of them fell by the overpowering enemy. Mrs. Helm, at that time only seventeen years of age, having been thrown from her horse at the commencement of the battle stood spell-bound

* This range of sand knolls was where Twelfth street strikes the lake, and was a noted landmark forty years ago, but has been graded down in making the street.

looking on at the scene of blood and carnage around, her. Her father and husband were engaged in the fearful strife, and she expected every moment to see them fall by the hand of murderous savages. As she stood awaiting her own fate a warrior with an uplifted tomahawk approached her, but dodging to one side the blow intended for the head took effect on the shoulder, producing a ghastly wound. She caught the savage around the neck and tried to get possession of his scalping-knife, which hung in a scabbard on his breast, but he threw her to one side, and was about to use his tomahawk on her head when she was caught in the arms of another Indian, who bore her off struggling into the lake. Here she was plunged under water, but her head frequently raised, so she soon discovered that the Indian did not intend to drown her. On looking into the face of the captor, although disguised with paint, she recognized Black Partridge, the well-known, trusty friend of her father's family. When the battle was over her protector conveyed his charge to the Indian camp and delivered her over to a friendly squaw, who dressed her wounds.

The night after the massacre a large body of hostile savages surrounded John Kinzie's dwelling with the intention of murdering the inmates, but by the timely interference of Black Partridge, assisted by

Shaubona and Sauganash, the would-be murderers were prevailed on to leave the house without accomplishing their bloody purposes, and thereby the lives of the family were saved.*

EMISSARIES FROM TECUMSEH.

About the first of October, 1812, two emissaries from Tecumseh, one of whom was a half-breed and the other a petty chief, came to Peoria for the purpose of enlisting warriors to take part in the impending conflict. A large body of Indians were encamped by the town, and they made an effort to induce the warriors to become allies of Tecumseh, and make war on the frontier settlements. They carried with them a quantity of worthless trinkets which they offered to those who would enlist, with a promise of a large amount of British gold on reaching the Wabash. Some of the young braves were in favor of going to war, also a few worthless half-breeds, who were too lazy to either work or hunt, imbibed the war spirit.

When the true mission of these visitors was made known to the citizens of Peoria they became very indignant, and decided to drive them out of town. Thomas Forsyth, Captain Maillet, with others, went to these emissaries and notified them to leave town

* Memories of Shaubona, page 23.

immediately, and if found there next day they would be arrested and put in prison. On being notified to leave, the recruiting party departed for other fields of labor, and the war spirit engendered by them soon died out.

These emissaries visited the homes of Gomo, Black Partridge, and other villages along the river, but met with no success. A messenger was sent from Peoria by Thomas Forsyth to all the neighboring villages, notifying the warriors of the intrigues of these visitors, and by this means their mission proved a failure.

UNJUST RETRIBUTION.

When emissaries sent by Tecumseh visited the different villages along the Illinois River, soliciting the chiefs to take part in the war, not one of them would have anything to do with it. Gomo and Black Partridge drove these agents, who were trying to enlist young warriors, away from their villages, and threatened them with death if they returned again. It is true some of the young braves took part in the Chicago massacre a few months before, but this was done contrary to the wish and command of the chiefs. The Indians having refused to take part in the war considered themselves at peace with all the world, and continued in their usual manner of living, spending their time in hunting, fishing, and with various kinds of amusements. While thus engaged in their daily avocations, unconscious of danger, an armed force was sent against them, as alleged, in retribution for past offenses.

In October, 1812, an army of two thousand Kentucky volunteers, commanded by General Hopkins, marched from Fort Harrison, on the Wabash, for the purpose of attacking the Indians along the Illinois River. This army, after two days' march, became frightened on seeing the prairie on fire, the soldiers mutinied, and refused to go further through a country full of fire and Indians, consequently they returned to Fort Harrison. About this time Governor Edwards with four hundred mounted rangers, commanded by Colonel Russell, marched to Peoria Lake, with the intention of joining Hopkins' army, but failing to find the army in the enemy's country, as they expected, they attacked and destroyed Black Partridge's village, killing about thirty Indians without losing a man. After burning the village the rangers with all haste returned to the settlement, as they were in an Indian country where a large number of warriors could be raised on short notice.

DESTRUCTION OF BLACK PARTRIDGE'S VILLAGE.

The following account of destroying Black Partridge's village is compiled from statement made to me many years ago by the "Old Ranger," General Samuel Whitesides, who was captain of a company in Governor Edwards' army, and well acquainted with all the facts.

The army, piloted by a half-breed, followed along the east side of Peoria Lake through the thick timber until they came within four miles of the village, and without a fire encamped here for the night. Early next morning Governor Edwards sent forward four young men, Thomas Carlin, afterward Governor of Illinois, with three of the Whitesides, for the purpose of reconnoitering, and this party found everything quiet at the Indian village. On the return of the scouts the troops were ordered forward in all haste to attack the enemy before they became aware of their presence, Captain Judy's company of spies leading the van, and having proceeded but a short distance when they suddenly came upon two Indians on horseback who raised their hands in token of submission. Captain Judy brought his rifle to his shoulder to fire on them, when some of the men begged for mercy, to which the captain replied he "did not leave home to take prisoners," and instantly the dust was seen to rise from the Indian's buckskin hunting shirt as the ball entered his body. The Indian fell from his horse with blood streaming from his mouth and nose, and in this condition commenced singing his death song. The rangers rode up to the dying Indian, who was reeling to and fro under the torture of pain, when all of a sudden he presented his rifle to shoot. The rangers sprang from their horses to escape the shot, but one of the party, a man named Wright. not being quick enough, received the charge in his body, producing a serious wound. The other Indian, who proved to be a squaw, sat on the horse spell-bound, making no attempt at defense or escape. Many shots were fired at her, at close range, none of which took effect, when she commenced crying, and was made a prisoner.

The Indians at the village were taken by surprise, as they had no warning of the approaching enemy, and were unprepared to make any resistance. Most of the warriors were off hunting, the squaws busy preparing breakfast, while the papooses were playing on the green, unconscious of approaching danger. The rangers putting their horses on a gallop rode into the village among the frightened Indians, shooting down all that came in their way, sparing neither the mother nor her infant, the aged or infirm, as these defenseless, panic-stricken people fled from their homes. The fugitives found refuge in a swamp near by where the horses of the pursuers mired down, and from this cause many of them owe the preservation of their lives. Some of the warriors having been wounded in the assault could not flee; these with small children, the aged and infirm, were slain in cold blood. The village with all its contents, as well as the corn in the caches, was burned, and the ponies, about one hundred in number, were taken by the rangers as trophies of war.

While the village was burning, and the rangers were having a jollification over their easy victory, an Indian of stately mien walked boldly along the bluff one hundred and fifty yards distant and fired his hun at them, after which he laughed long and loud, as he walked slowly away. Many shots were fired at him, without effect, and some of the rangers started in pursuit, but he succeeded in making his escape.

CHAPTER XXI.

LIEUTENANT HELM RANSOMED BY BLACK PARTRIDGE.

ABOUT two months after the Chicago massacre Black Partridge learned that Lieutenant Helm was still a prisoner among the Indians at a village on the Kankakee River. On receiving this intelligence he went to Peoria to consult with his friends in relation to his ransom. Captain J. B. Maillet, Antoine Des Champs and Thomas Forsyth were consulted, and by them it was agreed that Black Partridge should go immediately to the Indian village and try to procure the release of the prisoner. Presents were furnished by the three traders as a ransom for the captive, with a written order signed by Thomas Forsyth, and drawn on General Clark, Indian agent at St. Louis, for an additional one hundred dollars on his safe arrival at that place.

Black Partridge was provided with presents, and accompanied by a half-breed named Mark Topher, a resident of Peoria. When all the necessary arrangements were made the two travelers mounted their ponies and started off on a mission of mercy. On arriving at the Indian village they found the captive closely guarded by his captors, and still suffering from a wound received at the time of the massacre. When the old chief entered the lodge Lieutenant Helm threw his arms around his neck and cried like a child. He knew that Black Partridge had rescued his wife from a horrible death, and saved the lives of his father-in-law, John Kinzie, with his family, and in him he saw a prospect of his own liberation.

Black Partridge called the chiefs and warriors together and laid the presents before them, saying to them that all these articles, with additional one hundred dollars in silver, would be theirs by sending their prisoner to St. Louis to be liberated. After a long parley the Indians rejected the proposition, on the grounds that the ransom offered was not sufficient.

A short time before Captain Heald had been a prisoner of this band, and the Indians sent him to St. Joseph in charge of three warriors to be liberated. The pay received in exchange for him was so small that the warriors were sent back to reclaim their prisoner, but Captain Heald having been forwarded to Detroit they failed in the mission. Captain Heald and wife, both of whom were severely wounded, had left St. Joseph the day before the

Indians arrived, consequently they were compelled to return without their prisoner. Captain and Mrs. Heald were put into a bark canoe under the care of Robinson, a half breed, and taken to Mackinaw, three hundred miles distant, and delivered over to a British officer as prisoners of war.

The Indians refused to release their prisoner unless the ransom was increased; therefore Black Partridge offered them his pony, rifle, and a large gold ring which he wore in his nose. This proposition was accepted, and Lieutenant Helm, with Mark Topher, accompanied by a petty chief, all mounted on ponies, left the next day for St. Louis. Black Partridge accompanied the party on their way one day's journey, and then struck across the country for his village on the Illinois River.

It was late at night, very dark, and the rain poured down in torrents, as the old chief, on foot and alone, plodded his way through the thick river timber toward his village, where he expected to be warmly greeted by his family and friends, but he was doomed to disappointment. The village had disappeared, not a lodge, camping-tent, nor one human being could be found; nothing remained on its site but the charred poles of which the lodges were constructed. A pack of hungry wolves that had been feeding on the remains of the slain ran away at his approach, and their howling during the night added gloom and terror to the surrounding scene. The old chief drew his blanket around his body, and with sadness seated himself on the ground to await the approach of daylight. In the morning he found among the dead the remains of his favorite daughter with an infant son clasped in her arms, both cold in death. On the site of the village, and in the swamp near by, he found the dead bodies of many of his kindred and friends; among these was an old squaw of ninety winters, and also two of his grandchildren. All the dead were scalped, and some of the remains more or less mutilated.

MRS. BESSON'S NARRATIVE.

While in East St. Louis a short time ago I heard of an old lady by the name of Besson, who was one of the captives at the Chicago massacre, and is probably the only one now living. I called on this lady and listened to her thrilling narrative relating to past events, which to me was very interesting. She said her early recollections were associated with Chicago River, Lake Michigan and Fort Dearborn. By the side of the latter she had spent most of her childhood days, and gathered wild-flowers on the flat prairie now covered by the great metropolis of the west. Her maiden name was Mary Lee, a daughter of

Charles Lee, who with his family came to Fort Dearborn soon after it was built. Their dwelling stood on the beach of the lake, near the fort, and back of it was a small garden enclosed by a rail fence. For a number of years her father, Mr. Lee, was engaged in agricultural pursuits, selling the products of his farm at high rates to the occupants of the fort.

Mr. Lee made a large farm at a grove of timber on the south branch of Chicago River, four miles from its mouth, where Bridgeport now stands. The land near the lake being either wet or sandy rendered it unfit for farming purposes, which made it necessary to go up the river to make a farm, where the prairie was more rolling, and the soil rich. The communication between Lee's residence and his farm during most of the year was by a boat on the river, the intervening prairie much of the time being covered with water.

Mr. Lee built two cabins on his farm, and employed a number of persons to work the land. For some years the grove with its surroundings was known as "Lee's place," afterward called Hardscrabble, and at this place the Indians killed two persons, White and Devow, on the 7th of April, 1812, an account of which is given in Mrs. Kinzie's early history of Chicago.

At the time of the Chicago massacre Mr. Lee's family consisted of his wife ; an infant two months old ; his son, John of sixteen years ; Mary, now Mrs. Besson, the subject of our sketch, twelve; Lillie, ten ; and two small boys.

When the troops left Chicago for Fort Wayne Mr. Lee, with his family, accompanied them, taking with him all his horses, but leaving behind a large herd of cattle, which were shot by the Indians on the following day. Mrs. Lee, with her infant and two younger children, were in a covered wagon, while the two girls were on horseback, and all followed the army along the beach of the lake. Little Lillie was a handsome child, a great pet among the soldiers and traders about the fort, but she never before appeared so lovely as on the morning they left Chicago. She was mounted on a large gray horse, and to prevent her falling off or being thrown was tied fast to the saddle. She wore a white ruffled dress, trimmed with pink ribbon, a black jockey hat with a white plume on one side, and as her horse pranced and champed the bits at the sound of martial music little Lillie in a queenly manner sat in the saddle chatting gaily with her sister Mary, who rode by her side. As the soldiers threw kisses at her she would return them in her merry glee, chatting mirthfully with many of her acquaintances. Her young heart was made happy by the excitement of the morning, and she had no warning of the awful fate that awaited her a few minutes afterward.

Soon the guns of five hundred savages were raised against the troops, and by their murderous fire a large portion of the brave band were stricken down. During the battle little Lillie was wounded and fell from her seat, but still hung by the cord that bound her to the saddle. While in this perilous condition the frightened horse ran back and forth until caught by an Indian and the child rescued. When the battle was over Waupekee, a chief who had often been at Lee's house and trotted little Lillie on his knee, was much grieved to see her thus wounded, as he loved the child as though she were his own daughter. On examining Lillie's wound and finding it mortal the chief put an end to her suffering with a stroke of his tomahawk, saying afterward it was the hardest thing he ever did, but he could not bear to see her suffering. Mr. Lee and his son John were killed in the battle, and also the two young boys fell victims to the savages, while Mrs. Lee with her infant child and Mary were made prisoners. Mrs. Lee and infant fell into the hands of Waupekee, who had a village on the Des Plaines River about twenty miles from Chicago, who treated his prisoner kindly, and tried to induce her to marry him, notwithstanding he already had three wives. But she declined the marriage proposition, hoping some day to be ransomed and again restored to friends and civilization.

During the following winter Mrs. Lee's child became sick, and after all the known remedies of the Indian doctor failed to remove the disease the chief proposed to take it to Chicago for medical treatment. A Frenchman named Du Pin had taken possession of Kinzie's house soon after the burning of the fort, and for a number of years carried on a trade with the Indians.

On a cold day in the latter part of the winter Waupekee wrapped the sick infant in a blanket, mounted his pony, and with his charge started for Chicago. On arriving at Du Pin's residence the chief laid his package on the floor. "What have you there?" asked the trader; to which Waupekee replied, "A young raccoon, which I have brought you as a present;" and unwrapping the package there lay the sick infant almost smothered in the thick folds of the blanket. The trader made a prescription for the child, after which the chief carried it back to its mother, and it finally got well.

The trader became interested in the welfare of Mrs. Lee, and offered Waupekee a large amount of goods for his prisoner. This offer was accepted, the prisoner brought to the trading-house to be liberated, and soon afterward she became Madame Du Pin.

In the division of prisoners after the battle Mary Lee was taken to an Indian village on the Kankakee River, and in the following spring was carried to St. Louis, and ransomed by the Indian agent, General Clark. Some years afterward she married a Frenchman by the name of Besson, and is now living with a distant connection of her husband in East St. Louis.

Mary Lee never met her mother after that fatal day, and for many years supposed she was killed with the other members of the family, but subsequently learned of her captivity, liberation, marriage and death.

THE FRENCH AT PEORIA REGARDED AS ENEMIES.

While the inhabitants of Peoria were quietly pursuing their daily avocation of farming, hunting and trading with Indians, being as they supposed at peace with all the world, a plot was laid for their destruction. Being located in the midst of a wilderness country, nearly two hundred miles from the nearest American settlement, and having but little intercourse with the civilized world, they could not have known that war between the United States and

THE FRENCH AT PEORIA. 263.

England existed if they had not learned the fact from neighboring Indians.

Although the French at Peoria had lived within the jurisdiction of the United States government for twenty-four years they had never taken the oath of allegiance, acknowledged its power, nor paid tax to its support. They were a foreign people, speaking a different language, with habits and customs peculiar to themselves, and all their trade and intercourse was with the French citizens of Canada. The evil report in circulation about the French at Peoria assisting the Indians was believed by Governor Edwards, and he issued a proclamation calling for volunteers, in order to send an armed force against them. About two hundred men responded to the call, who were placed under the command of Captain Craig, and rendezvoused at Shawneetown. Four keel-boats were prepared, with rifle-ball-proof planking, mounted with cannon and filled with armed soldiers. The boats left Shawneetown early in October, and arrived at Peoria on the 5th of November. The inhabitants of Peoria were much surprised to see these four armed boats land at their wharf, as no large craft had ever reached that place before.

CAPTAIN CRAIG'S ACCOUNT OF HIS ATTACK ON PEORIA.

Captain Thomas E. Craig in his report to Governor Edwards, dated at Shawneetown, December 10, 1812, giving an account of the burning of Peoria, says: "I landed at Peoria on the 5th of November, and left it on the 9th. About midnight on the 6th the wind blew so hard on the lake that we were compelled to let the boats pass down into the river a short distance below the town. At daybreak next morning we were fired on by a party of Indians who had secreted themselves in the thick timber close by. Preparations were immediately made for battle, and bringing the cannons to bear we shelled the woods, but no enemy appeared, having fled after discharging their guns. Soon after daylight I had the boats landed opposite the center of the town, and took all the men prisoners, as they had undoubtedly pointed out our location to the Indians. I burned about half the town of Peoria, and would have burned all of it and destroyed all the stock but I expected General Hopkins' army to pass that way soon."

Part of the statements made by Captain Craig are undoubtedly true, but he fails to tell the whole story. The cold, selfish brutality practiced by the men under Captain Craig's command has never before been given to the public, and may appear strange to the reader, but it is nevertheless true. On this subject I have conversed with four different persons, Robert Forsyth, Rene La Croix, Hypolite Pilette, and Antoine Le Clair, all of whom were present at the time, being residents of Peoria. Their accounts of this affair will be found in the succeeding sketch, and are undoubtedly true, as all those statements agree on the principal facts, although differing somewhat in detail.

BURNING OF PEORIA.

The following account of the arrival of the gunboats, under command of Captain Craig, and burning of Peoria, are principally taken from the statements of Antoine Le Clair and Hypolite Pilette, both of whom were present at the time. Le Clair was a half-breed, and acquired much celebrity in after years as the proprietor of the city of Davenport, Iowa. Pilette is now living on the American Bottom not far from Prairie du Rocher, to whom many other references are made in this book.

On Sunday morning, November 5, 1812, while the people of Peoria were assembled at the church, engaged in saying mass, they were startled by the report of a cannon. The congregation, partly through fright and partly by curiosity, ran out of the church, when they discovered four armed boats in the lake under full sail. On coming opposite the town the boats rounded to, and landed at the wharf. Father Racine came down from the pulpit, and in his long black robe, with his bald head uncovered, started for the landing followed by all the congregation, men, women and children, where they met Captain Craig, who had landed from a boat. Thomas Forsyth, who spoke English, inquired of the captain the object of this visit, but the question was evaded, and in return he demanded of the citizens a supply of meat and vegetables for his men, which were furnished to them.

The soldiers landed from the boats, scattered through the town in search of plunder, and committed many depredations on the people. They broke open the store of Felix La Fontain, in which Antoine Le Clair was a clerk, and took therefrom two casks of wine and drank the contents. Some of the soldiers became intoxicated, forcing their way into houses, insulting women, carrying off eatables, blankets, and everything they took a fancy to. A soldier named Hitchcock, with three other armed men, went into a house occupied by very old people, and robbed it of most of its valuables. The jewelry and gold taken from this house were seen in the possession of the robbers on the following day, and a valuable watch with a heavy gold cross was exhibited afterward as trophies of war. It was long after dark before Captain Craig succeeded in getting his drunken, disorderly soldiers on board again, after which the boats were anchored out in the lake to prevent further depredations on the citizens. During the night a high wind arose, and to escape the waves in the lake the boats were run down into the channel, one-half mile below the town. About daybreak next morning eight or ten men went into the river timber to shoot beeves. The cattle being mixed with buffalo lived during the winter on the range, became partly wild, and hunted down in the woods same as deer or elk. This party of hunters attacked the herd in their lair, near where the gunboats lay, shot three beeves. and had commenced skinning them when the timber was riddled with cannon balls. The hunters left their beeves undressed, and fled for their homes without having the slightest idea why this hostile demonstration was made by the troops.

The boats were run up opposite the town immediately after the firing of cannon, when Captain Craig, with a large armed force, visited every house, and took all the men prisoners of war. Some of the men were still in bed, and not allowed time to dress, but hurried off to the boats with their clothes in their hands. A torch was applied to each house in town and burned with all their contents, while women and children with wild screams escaped from the burning buildings, and like a herd of frightened deer fled to a grove of timber above the desolated town. The church, which contained a golden image and a crucifix, with other valuable religious emblems, a present from the bishop of Quebec, were all burned with the building. The windmill, which stood on the bank of the lake, filled with grain and flour belonging to the citizens, was burned, as well as stables, barns, corn-cribs, etc. Felix La Fontain, Michael La Croix, Antoine Des Champs, and Thomas Forsyth, all of whom were traders with stores well filled with goods, were consumed by the flames. An old man named Benit, formerly a trader, had saved a large amount of gold by the toil of half a century, and had lain it away for old age. This gold was secreted in his dwelling, and finding it on fire he rushed in to save his treasure, and perished in the flames. The bones of this old man were found among the ashes of his dwelling in the following spring by a party of hunters who visited Peoria. Mrs. La Croix, a lady of refinement and personal attractions, who in after years became the wife of Governor Reynolds, being alone with her small children when her house was set on fire, appealed to the soldiers to save the clothing of herself and little ones, but their appeals were in vain, and with her children only escaped from the burning building.

There is an incident connected with the burning of Peoria not generally known, which to some extent explains the barbarous conduct of the soldiers, and somewhat palliates this outrage against humanity. About two months before Peoria was burned General Howard, stationed at Portage du Sioux, sent one of his soldiers, a young half-breed named Baptiste Snipkins, to Peoria in order to ascertain if the citizens were assisting the Indians in carrying on the war against the settlements, as had been reported. This messenger, called Howard's express by courtesy, but in fact a spy, learned all he could from the people without letting his true business be known. This young scapegrace instead of returning to the army, and reporting the true state affairs, according to orders, became enamored with a girl and prolonged his stay until the arrival of Captain Craig. To escape punishment for disobeying orders he reported to Craig's command that he was detained against his will, being a prisoner in the hands of the French, but this statement was afterward proven to be false. If this messenger had returned to the army and reported according to orders Craig's expedition would have been abandoned, and the destruction of Peoria averted.

A short time before Peoria was burned Thomas Forsyth had been appointed a government agent, but this appointment was kept a secret by the department at Washington, as it was thought if known it would lessen his influence with the Indians, and perhaps prejudice his townsmen against him. When Forsyth was made a prisoner he showed his commission to Captain Craig, containing the United States seal, but the incredulous officer pronounced it a forgery.

When the destruction of Peoria was completed the boats started down the river, carrying with them all the men as prisoners of war. Two miles below the present site of Alton, in the thick river timber, the prisoners were set at liberty, without tents, provision, or means of returning to their families.

Some of the women and children having been left at the burned town without food or shelter, were in a suffering condition, and without assistance would have perished. It was late in the fall, the sky overcast with gray clouds, and the cold November winds howled through the forest trees, blowing the dry leaves hither and thither. With high winds came squalls of snow, and the roaring and lashing of the waves in the lake caused mothers to draw infants closer to their bosoms to protect them from the inclement weather. To those destitute, helpless women all was dark and cheerless; the lamentations of mothers and cries of children were heard at a distance, and touched the heart of a sympathizing friend, although a savage. While in the midst of trouble they discovered a lone Indian walking leisurely along the beach of the lake, who with a firm step approached this group of women and children. He carried a rifle on his shoulder, a tomahawk and scalping-knife in his belt, and his face was painted in many colors. Notwithstanding he was disguised by paint, they recognized in the approaching Indian Gomo, a friendly chief, who had a village where Chillicothe now stands.

On the approach of the gunboats the inhabitants of Gomo's village fled westward, but the chief with two warriors secreted themselves in the thick timber watching the movements of the soldiers, and as soon as the boats departed down the river they came forth from their hiding place to assist their friends in distress. Gomo and his comrades furnished provision and shelter for the destitute women and children, and provided them with canoes to descend the river.

When furnished with an outfit for the journey the women with their little ones started down the river, camping each night on its banks, without tents to shelter them from the cold night air. After many days of toil, hardships and exposure, drenched by rain, suffering from cold and hunger, they reached Cahokia, where they were provided for by their countrymen, and afterward joined by their husbands and fathers.

It has been stated that Captain Craig took the women and children in the boat with the men, but this statement applies only to a few families. The families of Thomas Forsyth, Antoine Le Pance, Felix La Fontain, and perhaps one or two others, were put on board of the boats. But I am informed by Rene Le Croix and Hypolite Pilette that their mother's family, with many others, went down the river in bark canoes furnished by Gomo as previously stated.

Captain Craig has been much vilified for burning Peoria, but it must be remembered that he acted under the orders of Governor Edwards, who approved of his conduct, and afterward appointed him to an important office. It appears Governor Edwards was misled by false reports, which caused him to make war on innocent people, and in justice to his memory, I am willing to believe he did only what at the time he believed to be his duty.

DOMESTIC ANIMALS LEFT BY THE CAPTIVES.

The citizens of Peoria, when captured and carried off prisoners of war, left at their homes horses, cattle and hogs to run wild in the timber, and some of the former starved to death during the cold winter which followed. In the following spring a party of French and half-breeds belonging at Cahokia went to Peoria, gathered up the cattle, driving them south to the settlement, and returning some of these animals to their rightful owners.

Hogs ran wild in the river timber, and were found in large numbers ten years afterward by the early American settlers. As these hogs increased in numbers they scattered over the country, and were hunted down in the thick timber the same as deer.

In 1820 a wild bull and yearling heifer, crossed with buffalo, were shot by hunters in Spoon River timber. The Indians say at one time there was a large herd of wild cattle in this section of the country; but they hunted them down for beef. The wild cattle found by hunters, in all probability, were from the herd left at Peoria eight years before, or may have been the offspring of a herd that strayed away many years before, and became wild.

CHAPTER XXII.

INDIAN RAID ON THE SETTLEMENT.

SOME days after the destruction of Black Partridge's village, a party of warriors headed by the old chief returned to bury the dead, and found the remains of the slain scalped, mutilated, and partly devoured by wolves. After burying the dead the warriors engaged in a winter hunt, according to their custom, but Black Partridge traveled over the country in various directions, holding councils with chiefs and warriors, in order to enlist them in his cause. He was now old, his hair whitened by the snows of seventy winters, still his figure was erect and his step firm. Age had not dimmed the fire of his eyes, nor destroyed the valor of his youth. For many years he had been a friend of the whites, and to protect them from harm he had made many sacrifices. He had done everything in his power to prevent the massacre at Chicago, and saved the life of Mrs. Helm at the risk of his own. He had collected around him a few faithful friends to guard the dwelling of John Kinzie, and thereby rescued the family, with other prisoners, from massacre. He traveled a long way to the Kankakee village, gave his pony, rifle and ring to ransom Lieutenant Helm, and while tired and hungry returned to find his home desolated, and his friends murdered or driven away. Notwithstanding Black Partridge had made all these sacrifices for his white friends, they made war on him, burned his village, destroyed his corn, drove off his ponies, and killed about thirty of his people, among whom were some of his kinsmen, and he now lived only for revenge.

In the following summer, 1813, Black Partridge with about three hundred warriors, all mounted on ponies, left for the frontier settlement in the south part of the state. They went within thirty miles of the settlement, and secreted themselves in the thick timber of Shoal Creek, now in Bond county. From here they sent out small war parties to attack the settlers and kill defenseless women and children. The people became greatly alarmed at these depredations; many fled from their homes, and sought refuge at Cahokia or Kaskaskia; others built temporary forts to shield themselves from the tomahawks and scalping-knives of these ruthless savages. It is said a half-breed dressed as a white man acted as a spy, visiting different settlements under the pretext of hunting stray horses, and informed the

Indians of the most exposed points. Through this spy the Indians learned that an expedition was about to be sent against the villages on the Illinois River; so their camp was broken up, and they left for their homes.

CAPTIVITY OF AMANDA WOLSEY.

The descendants of some of the early settlers of St. Clair and Madison counties can give many thrilling narratives in relation to Indian raids during the late British war. Among other stories is the following narrative, which, on account of its romantic character, is worth preserving, and it is believed it has never before found its way into print.

In the spring of 1813 a man by the name of Joab Wolsey emigrated from Kentucky and made a claim in the Wood River settlement, about thirty miles northeast of Cahokia. The family of this emigrant consisted of a wife and four children, the eldest named Amanda, a girl of fifteen years of age, and of prepossessing appearance. Mr. Wolsey had built a cabin on his claim, in which his family were quartered, and was about to commence breaking prairie. His cabin occupied an exposed situation, being on the outskirts of the settlement, two or three miles from neighbors, but no one anticipated the great calamity which was about to overtake that little settlement on Wood River. On the afternoon of a bright spring day, while Wolsey was fixing his plow, and training his oxen, preparing to commence breaking prairie, a half-breed dressed in citizen's clothing called at the cabin and inquired about some horses which he said had strayed away. It was noticed that the stranger carried a large knife, with a navy pistol, in his belt, and his manner of looking around the premises caused Mrs. Wolsey to think that the visit of this stranger was for some evil purpose. On the night after the half-breed's visit, while all the family were asleep, the cabin was surrounded by Indians, Wolsey, his wife and three children killed, and the house set on fire. Amanda was made a prisoner, and held in the arms of a strong savage while she witnessed the murder of her parents, brothers and sisters, and their dwelling in flames. On the following day the mutilated remains of the victims were found, one of the children having been consumed in the cabin. On the same night three other families in the same settlement were attacked by Indians, many of the inmates slain, houses burned, and horses killed or stolen. Amanda Wolsey on becoming a prisoner was placed on an Indian pony, guarded by two warriors, and carried off a captive into the Indian country. The party having charge of the captive belonged to Waba band, who had a village on the south side of the Illinois River, almost opposite the outlet of Lake Depue. The Indians treated their prisoner with much respect, supplying her with a dress, and painting her face in accordance to Indian custom, and she associated with young maidens of her own age. She frequently accompanied the youths of both sexes to Starved Rock and neighboring villages, where they had dances and gay parties. A young chief fell in love with her, and proposed to make her his wife, but she repulsed his advances, looking forward to a time when she would be liberated and restored to friends and civilization. She had ofttimes thought of mounting a pony during the night when all were asleep and leaving for the settlement, but the great distance to be traveled, nearly two hundred miles, deterred her from this hazardous undertaking.

The summer had now passed, and the Indians were making preparations to leave their village for their annual hunt, when a messenger arrived in great haste, bringing the startling tidings that a large army had reached Peoria. This intelligence caused great excitement among the Indians, as their village was liable to be attacked at any moment. That night during the bustle and excitement Amanda escaped from the village, mounted a pony, and put it at the top of speed down the river in the direction of Peoria. But unfortunately her flight was discovered, and a number of warriors started in pursuit. The fugitive was overtaken in her flight, captured, carried back, and placed in close confinement. In December following a treaty of peace was made with the Indians, its conditions providing that all captives were to be liberated and returned to their friends. Under this treaty Amanda Wolsey was carried back to the settlement and set free.

GENERAL HOWARD'S EXPEDITION AGAINST THE INDIANS.

In September, 1813, General Howard, with an army consisting of five hundred regulars and nine hundred volunteers, marched against the Indians on the Illinois River. The regulars, commanded by Colonel Nichols, ascended the Illinois River in keelboats to Peoria Lake, and arrived there some days in advance of the volunteers, who were mounted and came aross the country.

The Indians having received an intimation that an army was about to be sent against them became very much alarmed, and most of them were in favor of making overtures for peace. Black Partridge, the leading spirit of the war party, was in favor of defending themselves against the aggression of the whites, but he could not enlist the different bands in his scheme. Shaubena, Waba and Waubonsie, with many of their braves, were with Tecumseh, and warriors of the different bands could not be united under any one chief. Senachwine was opposed to war, and being a chief of great influence, gifted with stirring eloquence, carried with him a large portion of the warriors.

Black Partridge was grave and morose, brooding over the wrongs he had received from the whites the year before, and now lived only for revenge. Notwithstanding he had taken many scalps the past summer, and murdered defenseless women and children, he still thirsted for more blood.

The largest village in the country, called Wappa, was located on Bureau Creek, eight miles from the river, and on the present site of Tiskilwa. The head chief of this village, named Comas, was a son-in-law of Black Partridge, and here the old chief found a home after the destruction of his village.

BLACK PARTRIDGE WITH HIS BRAVES IN DEFENSE OF THEIR COUNTRY.

On a bright, warm day in the early part of Indian summer the warriors at Comas' village were lounging along the creek, some fishing, others running foot races, wrestling, or playing with balls, hoops, etc. All was quiet; neither war parties, dances, religious feast nor marriage celebration, nothing whatever to relieve the monotony of village life. A party of warriors was about to start west on a hunt when two scouts arrived with the startling intelligence that troops had arrived at Peoria, and were engaged in building a fort. On receiving these tidings Black Partridge mounted his pony, riding back and forth through the village calling for volunteers to accompany him to victory. A large number of warriors responded to the call, and mounted upon ponies, armed and equipped for war, were soon on their way to meet the enemy. On their way they stopped at Senachwine and Crow's villages in order to obtain recruits, but were unsuccessful, as no warriors of either village would join this war party. On reaching Gomo's village they found the chief and many of the warriors off on a hunt, and but few of those at home were willing to engage in this hazardous enterprise. Black Partridge was much discouraged by his failure to raise a large force, as he expected, but with his little band of braves, amounting to about three hundred, he concluded to give immediate battle before the enemy could erect fortifications for their defense.

While the troops under Colonel Nichols were engaged in building a block house, unconcious of danger, they were attacked by Black Partridge's band of warriors, and had it not been for persons outside of the picket guards giving timely alarm in all probability a bloody battle would have resulted.

COLONEL DAVENPORT'S ACCOUNT OF AN ATTACK ON THE BLOCK HOUSE.

For incidents relating to an attack on the block house, building a fort, and treaty with the Indians, I am indebted to Colonel George Davenport, a noted Indian trader at Rock Island who was murdered July 4, 1845, by the "bandits of the prairie."

Mr. Davenport, at that time a young man, was an uncommissioned officer in Captain Owen's company, of the regular army, and in that capacity served during the war.

On arriving at Peoria Lake the soldiers commenced building a block house for storing the baggage, as well as a protection against an attack from the enemy. A well having been dug near the block house to supply it with water, it became necessary to have a sweep to draw it; consequently Mr. Davenport, with two companions, went into the woods to get a grapevine for that purpose. Having found one suitable, Davenport climbed the tree to cut it off, and while doing so he discovered a large body of Indians skulking in the timber, going in the direction of the block house. On seeing this war party Davenport and his companions gave an alarm, and in all haste fled toward the block house, but finding Indians in that direction turned their course for the gunboats, which were moored in the lake. With all speed the fugitives ran for the boats, closely followed by the Indians, who fired at them many shots, while yelling like demons. The soldiers on the gunboats, thinking only of their own safety, pushed them off from the shore, but fortunately one of them grounded on a sand bar, which was the means of saving the lives of Davenport and his companions. The fugitives rushed into the water waist deep, pushed the grounded boat off, and jumped on board of it, while the Indians fired on them, many of the rifle balls whizzing by their heads and lodging in the side of the vessel. The boats went off some distance from the shore, nevertheless the Indians continued to fire on them, but without effect. A cannon on one of the boats was brought to bear on the savages, but in the excitement of the moment its muzzle was raised above the port-hole, and the ball tore off a portion of the side of the vessel. The Indians also attacked the block house, which was in an unfinished condition, but met with a warm reception from those within. The cannons on the boats having been brought to bear on the Indians, they fled from the thick timber where they had taken shelter, and the fight ended.

CHAPTER XXIII.

BUILDING OF FORT CLARK.

GENERAL HOWARD with nine hundred mounted volunteers left their quarters at Portage des Sioux in September, 1812, and followed up the Mississippi to the present site of Quincy, and from here crossed the country to Peoria. The troops encamped on the site of the old French town, and a strong picket guard placed around the encampment to prevent being surprised by the Indians. During the night an alarm was given, and a report circulated through the camp that they were about to be attacked by a large body of Indians. All the troops were under arms, many shots fired at phantoms, and one soldier killed by a sentinel, but the alarm proved to be false, as no enemy could be found.

On the following day, after the arrival of this army, by order of the commander it marched up to Gomo's village, at the head of the lake, but found it deserted, and after burning the town and destroying the corn in the fields returned to Peoria.

Preparations having been made to build a fort on the site of the old French town for the purpose of holding possession of the country, timbers were cut on the opposite side of the lake, and floated across to build block store-houses, and enclose them with palisades. On a high piece of ground near the bank of the lake a fort was built, consisting of stockades made of two rows of split timbers, and the space between them filled with dirt. A ditch surrounded the fort, and at two corners were bastions for mounting cannon. Inside of the stockades was a large block-house, two stories high, and on three sides of it were port-holes, so the inmates could fire on the enemy in case of an attack. Besides this block-house were store-houses, and quarters for officers and soldiers.

When the fort was completed and cannons mounted on its ramparts, with flags waving on each bastion, General Howard ordered all the soldiers on duty, forming in double file, fronting the gateway.

A speech was made by the commanding officer, drums beat, soldiers cheered, the cannons fired a salute, and with much enthusiasm the fort was dedicated and named "Fort Clark" in honor of General George Roger Clark, the hero of Kaskaskia and Vincennes.

GUNBOATS ASCEND THE RIVER TO THE RAPIDS.

Four keel-boats, mounted with cannon and filled by armed soldiers belonging to the regular army, under command of Major Christy, ascended the river from Peoria in search of the enemy. These boats landed at different villages along the river, but found them all deserted, the Indians having fled from their homes. These villages were burned with all of their contents, and the corn in the fields, and pelts, furs and other valuables stored away in the caches were also destroyed or carried off.

On Hickory Ridge, below the mouth of Bureau Creek, the Indians, headed by Black Partridge, tore down the two cabins built many years before by De Beuro, and with these logs erected a breastwork on the river so they could fire on the boats while ascending the stream; but on finding these boats protected by heavy plank, rifle proof, with portholes for cannon, the warriors fled without firing a gun or letting their presence be known.*

Major Christy intended to ascend the Illinois as far as the mouth of Fox River, but finding it difficult to pass the rapids he landed at Starved Rock. On the following day the boats were started down stream,

---

*Colonel G. S. Hubbard says when he came to the country, in 1818, this breastwork was still standing, and its relics, consisting of a pile of rotten logs, could be seen in the early settlement of the country.

landing at the mouth of Bureau Creek, and from here a war party, commanded by Lieutenant Robenson, went out in search of the enemy.

INDIANS COLLECT ON BUREAU.

When the troops under General Howard reached Peoria the inhabitants of Gomo's, Senachwine, Crow and other towns fled from their homes and collected at Comas' village, on Bureau Creek. Here they intended to make a stand, await the approach of the invaders, and fight for their country and homes. All the squaws and papooses, with the aged warriors unable to bear arms, were sent up the creek about seven miles above the town, where they were secreted in the thick timber.*

At Comas' village were collected about one thousand warriors, occupying all the lodges, while above

---

* About two miles northwest of Princeton, in the valley of Bureau, is a singular narrow ridge, about sixty feet high, extending from the east bluff part way across the bottom. This remarkable ridge, which looks like a freak of nature, is called Back Bone, and on top of it now passes a public road. With the Indians this place became a noted landmark, and it was equally so with hunters in the early settlement of the country.

Immediately north of the Back Bone, in the thick bottom timber by the side of a spring, was an old Indian camping-ground, and here their camp poles stood long after they left the country. In the fall of 1836 a party of Indian hunters were encamped here for a number of weeks, having returned from the west to visit the home of their youth. Among these Indians was one who spoke good English, and while in conversation with him I obtained many of the items narrated in this chapter. He said at the time of the war many thousand squaws and papooses were encamped on this ground, and here Madas, a noted warrior, and brother of Black Partridge, died from a wound received in the fight at Peoria a few days before, and he showed me his grave on the Back Bone, which was surrounded by a pen built of small timbers or poles.

and below it the meadow was covered with camping-tents. On the bottom prairie below the village many hundred ponies were feeding, all of them spanceled so they could be caught and mounted at a moment's notice. It was expected that Howard's army would follow up the river and attack them in their retreat, therefore a suitable place to make a defense was selected. This was in the thick timber some distance below the village, where they could fire on the invaders while crossing a small bottom prairie.

Indian scouts, who were all the while on the alert, discovered the troops ascending the river in boats, and in all haste conveyed the tidings to the village. On receiving these tidings the drums beat to arms, all was bustle and excitement, and in a short time the warriors were secreted in their ambuscade awaiting the approach of the enemy, but when they found that the boats continued on up the river they returned to their village.

LIEUTENANT ROBENSON IN SEARCH OF THE ENEMY.

About eighty soldiers, under the command of Lieutenant Robenson, left the gunboats on the river and marched up Bureau Creek, with the intention of visiting Comas' village, situated eight miles distant, on the present site of Tiskilwa. After going up the valley about five miles through timber and prairie they discovered a trail with fresh pony tracks. On making this discovery they came to a halt for consultation on the propriety of continuing their march, knowing that they were near a large Indian village, and at any point of timber were liable to fall into an ambuscade of lurking savages. Some were in favor of going on and burn the village, if vacated, but fortunately a majority opposed it; consequently they turned about and retraced their steps back to the river.

On the return of Robenson's command with the report of no Indians found, Major Christy came to the conclusion that they had fled from the country, and preparations were made to descend the river. Before leaving cannons fired a salute, toasts were drank, and the stream named Robenson's River, which name it continued to bear for many years afterward, and so appeared on all the early maps of the state.

Indian scouts had watched the keel-boats as they ascended and descended the river, and on seeing them land at the mouth of the creek, and preparing to send out troops to make observations, they put their ponies on a gallop to convey the tidings back to the village, and it was the tracks of their ponies which Robenson's party discovered while on their march. On learning of the approach of troops warriors mounted their ponies and rode in all haste to the place selected to attack the invaders. Here many of the warriors secreted themselves in the thick timber, while those mounted remained in the rear to intercept the vanquished troops. Had Robenson's command continued their march toward the village, the probabilities are but few of them would have escaped death, as the warriors outnumbered them five to one, and many of them mounted, while the soldiers were on foot.

TREATY OF PEACE—THE WAR ENDED.

Black Partridge and his friends finding it impossible to unite the different bands so as to continue the war successfully, thought it best to make overtures for peace, and accordingly a large delegation of chiefs and warriors went to Fort Clark for that purpose. When this party arrived within a few miles of the fort they came to a halt, when Senachwine, accompanied by two warriors carrying white flags, went forward to the gate of the fort, and prepared to meet the commanding officer in council. Arrangements were made for meeting in council on the following day, for the purpose of agreeing on terms of peace. At the appointed time about forty chiefs and warriors, decorated with eagle and turkey feathers, made their appearance, and were met by General Howard and all the officers of his command. After shaking hands and passing around the pipe of peace, Senachwine made a speech before the council, in which he said they had come to make peace with the whites and forever bury the tomahawk. In reply to this speech General Howard said he had no power to treat with them, but proposed to conduct their head chiefs to St. Louis, and General Clark, the general agent, would hear their propositions for peace. The Indians agreed to this, and a delegation of thirteen chiefs and one squaw were selected to go to St. Louis. Among these chiefs were Black Partridge, Senachwine, Comas, Shick-Shack, Crow and Gomo. General Howard ordered George Davenport to select four trusty men and escort these Indians to St. Louis. All necessary arrangements having been made, this party on the following day went on board of a pirogue and started down the river for St. Louis. It being late in December the weather was cold; consequently after one day's journey the river froze up, and the remainder of the distance was made on foot. The pirogue was secreted in the thick timber, together with part of their stores, including a keg of whiskey, when the travelers, with such baggage as they could carry, proceeded on their way. At night both whites and

Indians camped together, but each party kept a guard on duty, as they feared treachery.

This party after five days' travel arrived safe at St. Louis; a treaty of peace was concluded, and the Indians left five of their number as hostage for its fulfillment. The Indians on their return were escorted as far as Alton above the settlement, and they returned to their homes.

After a treaty of peace with the Indians Fort Clark was abandoned, the troops returned to the settlement, and the volunteers discharged from service.

CHAPTER XXIV.

DESCENDANTS OF FRENCH SETTLERS AT PEORIA.

OF the descendants of French residents who were born at Peoria, and remember incidents connected with its destruction, only three are now living (if we except Mrs. Chandler, daughter of Michael La Croix), and they are now far advanced in life. A short time ago I visited these three persons, and listened to an account of their early recollections of Peoria, as well as the traditions of their ancestors. One of these descendants, Robert Forsyth, a man of wealth and enterprise, lives on a farm six miles west of St. Louis.* He is a son of Thomas Forsyth, a trader and Indian agent at Peoria at the time it was burned, and for many years after an agent of the Sacs and Foxes at Rock Island. Mr. Forsyth was of Irish lineage, a half-brother of John Kinzie, of Chicago, and the early part of his life was spent among the French and Indians at Peoria. He was one of the claimants for the land on which the city of Peoria now stands, and his son Robert (above re-

* Died since writing the above.

ferred to) prosecuted these claims against the occupants, and obtained from them a large sum of money.

Major Thomas Forsyth for nearly twenty years was employed by the government as an Indian agent, and he is frequently referred to, both in General Clark's and governors' dispatches to the secretary of war. He appears to have been the only American-born citizen in the west, at that time, with whom the Indians had confidence, and chiefs of various tribes continued to counsel with him until the time of his death, which occurred at St. Louis October 29, 1833.

In reference to the burning of Peoria Major Forsyth made an entry in his journal which contains the following language: "A band of ruffians from Shawneetown, commanded by Captain Thomas E. Craig, took us prisoners as though we were malefactors, and set us adrift on the bank of the Mississippi, near where Savage's ferry now is. Many poor unfortunate persons with wives and small children had not a change of clothing nor a blanket to protect them from the cold winds."

Rene La Croix, another of the descendants of the Peoria French, lives in Belleville, and like Robert Forsyth made money out of the French land claims. His father, Michael La Croix, married Catherine

Dubuque, cousin of Julian Dubuque, a noted pioneer and founder of the city in Iowa which still bears his name. La Croix came to Peoria in 1805, and for many years was engaged in trade, shipping furs to Canada in a two-mast batteau, and loading back with goods for the Indian market. He was on his way to Canada with his batteau, loaded with furs, when the town was destroyed, and on arriving at Montreal heard that the Yankees had burned Peoria, and killed all its inhabitants, among whom were his wife and children. With his heart filled with revenge he joined the British army, became an officer, and took part in many of the battles which followed. At the close of the war La Croix learned that his family were not killed, as reported, but living at Cahokia, consequently he came west to join them. A few years after joining his family he died, and his widow married John Reynolds, afterward Governor of Illinois.

Hypolite Pilette, a descendant of the Peoria French, is a son of Louis Pilette, one of the French land claimants, born at Peoria in 1799, and is now living on the American Bottom. He claims to be a great-grandson of Captain Richard Pilette, who in 1686 built Le Fort des Miamies, on Buffalo Rock, and has now in his possession the sword, eagle and epaulets worn by that distinguished personage. In speaking of the burning of Peoria by Captain Craig, in 1812, he said: "On a cold November morning, when a boy of thirteen years of age, I was driven from home without coat, hat or shoes; my mother sick with the ague, and with an infant in her arms, was compelled to leave her bed, protected from the cold winds only by an Indian blanket, while our house with all its contents were consumed by the flames. My father a prisoner, my mother sick, my brothers and sisters almost naked, without food or shelter, we were left to our fate. Thus were we turned out of doors to freeze and starve, but fortunately rescued by friendly Indians."

Three days after Peoria was burned Mrs. Pilette, with her five small children, were put in a canoe by the Indian chief Gomo, and in company with others as unfortunate as herself started down the river. After six days of exposure, and suffering from cold and hunger, they reached Cahokia, and were provided for by their countrymen and friends. Pilette is a jolly old Frenchman, fond of a bottle of wine, and very talkative while under its influence. Although born and raised in Illinois he speaks no English except in broken, detached sentences, but in his own language, I should judge, he is quite eloquent. While speaking of the past Pilette became very much excited; his eyes flashed with anger, his voice raised to a high key, while denouncing the barbarous acts of Captain Craig, and from that time, said he, "I hate Yankees."

There are some facts connected with the burning of Peoria not generally known, but when properly understood will explain a matter which to many appears mysterious. A few months ago I called on an old gentleman living in St. Louis, by the name of James Porter, who was a soldier in Captain Craig's command. Mr. Porter believes that he is the only person now living who participated in burning Peoria, and although seventy years have passed away he has a vivid recollection of many of the incidents which occurred on that eventful day. He says all the soldiers believed that the French were assisting the Indians to make war on the settlers, and this belief was confirmed by Baptiste Snipkins, General Howard's express, who came on board of a boat as soon as they arrived at Peoria.

Mr. Porter also says that it was afterward ascertained that the depredation on the settlement was committed by a war party of Sacs and Foxes, and the Indians along the Illinois River were innocent as well as the French. When all the facts became known, years after Peoria was burned, Captain Craig and many of those under his command were filled with remorse on account of having committed this outrage on innocent people.

PERILS OF FUR TRADERS ON ILLINOIS RIVER.

After the burning of Peoria there was but little trade on the Illinois River for three years, and the Indians failing to obtain their usual supply of goods were in a suffering condition. For an American trader to enter the Indian country would be at the risk of his life, and while French traders were safe from harm among the Indians, they were liable to fall into the hands of soldiers, and have their goods confiscated to the government. After the evacuation of Fort Dearborn a Frenchman named Du Pin took possession of John Kinzie's dwelling, and for three years traded with the Indians. During the continuation of the war a number of Frenchmen continued to live with the Indians, but none of them except Du Pin kept a stock of goods for Indian trade.

In the summer of 1814 Jacques Jarret, a French Canadian, came down the Illinois River in a batteau loaded with goods for the Indian market. The trader had two Frenchmen employed as boatsmen, and an Englishman named John Ford acted as a clerk and salesman. At different places where the batteau stopped to trade the Indians looked on Ford with much suspicion, accused him of being an American, and at one time threatened him with death. While the batteau lay at the mouth of Crow Creek, for the purpose of trade, a large number of warriors collected around Ford, denounced him as an American and a spy, and made him a prisoner, and were about to carry him off to a place of execution. In vain Jarret tried to make the warriors understand that Ford was an Englishman, and that his country was then at war with the Americans. After a long parley the prisoner was ransomed by the trader giving the captors a large amount of goods for his liberation. After this narrow escape from death Ford laid aside his fashionable suit, clothed himself as a boatman, and disguised his face with paint. From that time he spoke no language in the presence of Indians, and was known thereafter among them as the deaf and dumb Frenchman.

BURNING OF FORT CLARK.

For many years this old historical spot at the foot of the lake was known as Fort Clark, but as the town became a place of importance it again resumed its former name, "Peoria." At the close of the British war the Chauteaus and Menards continued the fur trade along the Illinois River until superseded by the American Fur Company. In 1816 Antoine Des Champs received an appointment of general agent of the American Fur Company in Illinois territory. Des Champs was an old fur trader, at one time a resident of Peoria, but afterward at Cahokia, and proved to be an efficient agent. He dispatched runners to different Indian villages, requesting the inhabitants to meet him at Fort Clark on the 5th of August to receive presents sent them by the great fur company. At the appointed time about one thousand Indians were collected at the old fort when Des Champs arrived with a Mackinaw boat loaded with goods. After making many presents to the Indians, and obtaining their promise to patronize the new fur company, he establishing trading-posts at various places along the river.

It has already been stated that Fort Clark was built in the fall of 1813, abandoned soon after, and never occupied by troops again. No white person lived in Peoria (then called Fort Clark) after the troops left it until the spring of 1819. The gate of the fort having been left open it became a lair for deer, and a roost for wild turkeys. In the fall of 1816 a party of hunters from St. Clair county came to Fort Clark and found about twenty deer in the fort, and the floors of the block-houses covered with manure. The hunters cleaned out this building, and occupied it as a residence during a stay of ten days while hunting deer and collecting honey in the river timber. Fort Clark stood unmolested until the fall of 1818, when it was burned by the Indians.

The following account of the burning of Fort Clark is taken from the statements of Colonel Gurdon S. Hubbard, now a resident of Chicago:

In the fall of 1818 Antoine Des Champs, general agent of the American Fur Company, accompanied by a number of persons, were on their way to St. Louis with two boats loaded with furs. On coming around a point in the lake they discovered Fort Clark on fire, and near it were about two hundred Indians engaged in a war dance. The warriors, almost naked, hideously painted, as they went through the dance yelled like demons. They had a large number of scalps hanging to their belts, and in one part of the dance these were placed on the ends of spears and held above their heads, after which they went through the motions of taking them from the heads of the victims. Des Champs was well acquainted with many of the Indians, and went among them engaged in conversation, leaving the boats guarded by one of his men and Mr. Hubbard, who at that time was a boy of sixteen years of age. The Indians inquired of Des Champs about this boy, who in reply said that he was his adopted son from Montreal, but they did not credit this statement, saying he looked like an American, and regarded him with suspicion. An Indian took a scalp from his belt, and held it near Hubbard's face, saying to him that it was taken from the head of his countryman. Young Hubbard became very much frightened, but when the Indian urinated on the scalp, and with it sprinkled his face, all fear vanished, and picking up a gun which lay in the bottom of the boat fired at the Indian, but the man in charge of the boat threw up the muzzle as it went off, thereby saving the Indian's life. This affair created great excitement, and Des Champs fearing trouble bade his Indian friends good-by, went aboard of the boats, and continued on his way down the river.

Although the block-houses and part of the stockades of Fort Clark were burned, as above stated, a portion of the latter stood for many years after. In the spring of 1819 a party of the emigrants from Clinton county, among whom were Captain Abner Eads, Isaac and Josiah Fuhlton and J. Hersey, came to Fort Clark, and from that time dates the American settlement here. These emigrants pitched their tents against the stockades of the old fort, and for years the inclosure within the pickets was used for penning cattle. During the Black Hawk war, in 1832, the old fort was repaired, new pickets put in place of burned ones, and intended as a place of protection from an attack of Indians.

GENERAL INDEX.

American Bottom - - - - - 183
American Pioneers of Illinois - - - 206
Antiquities of Illinois - - - - 17
Aztalan the ruined city - - - - - 197
A scene of horror - - - - - - 75

Besiegers and besieged - - - - - 155
Bourassa, Colonel Joseph N. cited - - 160
Brady's Tom wild adventure - - - - 119
Baptiste Jean and Father Bonner- - - 212
Baldwin Elmer cited - - - - 201–202
Black Partridge, a noted Indian chief - - 242
    Saves the life of Mrs. Helm - - - 245
    Destruction of his village - - 251
    In defense of his country - - - 280
Besson's Mrs. narrative - - - - 257
Bruce Elijah a vagabond - - - - - 239
Bucher's Father Jacques manuscript - - 117
Buffalo disappearance of - - - - - 209
Burning of Peoria - - - - - 265

Chicago, early history of - - - - 210
Chassagoac, an Indian chief - - - 101
Clark, Colonel G. R. conquest of Illinois - 127
Cross raised on the bank of Chicago River - 38
Chartres Fort - - - - - - - 180
Cahokia - - - - - - - 186
Chauteau Auguste and Pierre mentioned - 202
Costumes and manners of the French - 222

304   GENERAL INDEX.

Council at Cahokia - - - - - - 234
Craig's Captain attack on Peoria - - 264

De Beuro Pierre an Indian trader - - - 229
Domestic animals left by the captives - - 273
Davenport, Colonel George - - - - 282
Descendants of French settlers at Peoria - 293
Des Champs Antoine mentioned - - - 301

English and French relation with Indians - 205
Edwards Governor Ninian mentioned - - 237

Fort Crève-Cœur - - - - - 57
Fort St. Louis building of - - - - 83
    Attacked by Iroquois - - - 87
    Burned - - - - - - - 99
    Relics of - - - - - - 173
    French settlement at - - - - 104
Fox River the ruined fort of - - - 201
French inhabitants of Peoria - - - - 222
French land claims - - - - - 226
False report circulated - - - - - 239
French at Peoria - - - - - - 262
Fort Clark, building of - - - - - 284
    Burning of - - - - - 299

Ghastly spectacle - - - - - - 163
Gold, searching for - - - - - 168
Goodell Dr. J. H. referred to - - - 201
Gabriel, Father death of - - - - 73

History, errors of - - - - - - 173
Hitt, Colonel D. F. cited - - 173–176–201
Helm, Lieutenant ransomed - - - - 254
Heald Captain mentioned - - - - 255
Howard's General expedition - - - - 279
Hubbard Colonel G. S. cited - - -

GENERAL INDEX.   305

Illinois topography of River - - - - 22
    Early French settlement of - - 112
    British rule of - - - - - 117
    Early government of - - - 207
Indians Illinoisans - - - - - - 24
    Massacre of — - - - 25
Iroquois raid of - - - - - - 26
    Tribes in Illinois territory - - 193
    Drepredations of - - - - - 232
    Council on Bureau - - - - 247
    Trade with - - - - - - 85

Joliet Louis mentioned - - - - 30
Jennette Medore, a fur trader - - - 202

Kennedy Pat searching for copper - - 125
Kaskaskia - - - - - - - 187
Kaskaskia and Cahokia Indians - - - 189
Kinzie John mentioned - - - - - 244

La Vantum or great Illinois town - - 47
    Voyageurs at - - - - - 34
    French at - - - - - - 62
La Pance Felix cited - - - - - 49
La Salle and friends western bound - - 53
    In an Indian camp - - - - 59
    Success, failure and death - - - 86
Le Fort des Miamis - - - - - 93
Louisiana colony - - - - - - 102
Le Rocher - - - - - - - 171
La ville de Maillet - - - - - 218
Lee Charles noticed - - - - - 258

Marquette Jacques - - - - - 28
    Death of - - - - - - 43
    Resurrecting his bones - - - 45
Mammoth and Mastodon - - - - 20
Massac Fort of - - - - - - 20

GENERAL INDEX.

Marseilles, ancient fortification at - - - 199
Mississippi River, discovery of - - - 30
Mission of Immaculate Conception - - - 40
Monks of La Trappe - - - - - 194

Old fort near Starved Rock - - - - 195

Peoria Lake of - - - - - 56
    Burning of - - - - -
    Indians - - - - - 191
Pilette Captain Richard mentioned - - - 93
    Hypolite mentioned - - - -
Pontiac - - - - - - 137
    Assassinated - - - - 147
Prairie du Rocher - - - - - 185
Porter James mentioned - - - - 297

Relics of French and Indians - - - - 174
Relics of a tragedy - - - - 166
Rock of refuge - - - - - 142
Retribution unjust - - - - - 249
Robinson Lieutenant in search of the enemy - 288

St. Louis, early settlement of - - - 99
St. Joseph expedition against - - - - 123
Starved Rock - - - - - - 78

Tecumseh at Peoria - - - - 231
    Emissaries from - - - - 248
Tidings of war - - - - - 243
Territory of Illinois at the time of the British war - - - - - - - 243
Treaty of peace - - - - - 280
Torturing prisoners - - - - - 72
Tonti de Henri - - - - - 70
    Return of his victorious army - - 90
    Death of - - - - - 96

Wolsey's Amanda captivity - - - 276

www.ingramcontent.com/pod-product-compliance
Lightning Source LLC
Chambersburg PA
CBHW032047230426
43672CB00009B/1498